Late Breaking News

OTHER TITLES BY DR. LEONARD

The Promise of His Coming: Interpreting New Testament State-ments Concerning the Time of Christ's Appearance (with J. E. Leonard). Laudemont Press, 1996.

A Theological Miscellany (Ghost Writer). W Publishing (Thomas Nelson), 2005.

Silence of the Drums: A Christian Family in the Midwest Deals with End-Time Issues. Xulon Press, 2005.

Heart of the Highriders: In a Fantasy World, Seekers Find the True Source of Good (with Charity R. Silkebakken). Word Association Publishers, 2006.

New America: A Novel. Lampstand Books, 2009.

The Big Picture: A Christian Couple Explores the "Prosperity Gospel" (with Shirley Anne Leonard). Lampstand Books, 2013.

LATE BREAKING NEWS

Reconsidering the Gospel of the New Testament

Richard C. Leonard, Ph.D.

LAUDEMONT PRESS
HAMILTON, ILLINOIS

© 2018 Laudemont Press
P.O. Box 369, Hamilton, Illinois 62341
www.laudemont.org
ISBN (USA) 978-1-884454-08-0

Contents

Chapter 1
Late Breaking News

We're all familiar with the newscast scenario when the anchor interrupts the sequence of reports with "This just in . . . late breaking news . . ." Something has happened that's important enough to break into the daily cycle of reporting.

Usually, in our experience, what's "just in" is a report of something that's not good — an earthquake, a shooting, an international incident, the latest financial crisis, the downfall of some prominent figure. It's no wonder many people have a negative view of the network or cable news, because so much of it is . . . well, negative.

But there can be good news, too. The cessation of World War II hostilities, the development of the polio vaccine, and the fall of the Berlin wall are examples of "breaking news" most people would welcome. Good things are occurring all the time, but sadly they often go under-reported.

Other examples of what's supposed to be "good news" are found in the world of advertising. Every TV commercial proclaims the advantages of the vendor's product. The newest model of our car can span desert wastes, climb rocky crags, hold your family of five with all your luggage — and do all that using less fuel. The latest pharmaceutical from our company

7

can relieve your medical condition so you can enjoy romping on the beach or spending time with your grandchildren (if it doesn't kill you first from the side effects).

The ancient Greeks had a word for this "good news" that makes a beneficial difference in your life. They called it *euangelion*, the announcement of an occurrence that has changed the course of history. Because of this world-changing event this evangel, this "gospel" or good news, must be proclaimed to all whose existence will be affected by it.

So, in the Mediterranean world of ancient Rome, a certain "gospel" went forth: because of the victory and the benevolent rule of one man, there will be peace and prosperity and progress for all who come under his authority. So pervasive was this *euangelion* that people came to hail that man as lord, savior, and even as the son of the divine.

That man was Caesar, the *imperator* or emperor of Rome. As each Caesar succeeded the one before, the new emperor proclaimed his predecessor to be divine — which made the current ruler the son of a god. The worship of Caesar spread throughout the empire; sacrifices to him were required on public occasions, along with all the obligatory offerings to local divinities such as Artemis in Ephesus. Caesar didn't mind if you sacrificed to these other divinities as long as he received his due. And woe to anyone who dared refrain from taking part in these rites exalting the lord, the savior, and the son of the gods.

How remarkable, then, that the apostle Paul, at the beginning of his letter to the Christians ("Messiah-people") of Rome, could speak of God's "good news"

> which he promised beforehand through his prophets in the holy Scriptures, concerning his Son, who

was descended from David according to the flesh and was declared to be the Son of God in power according to the Spirit of holiness by his resurrection from the dead, Jesus the Messiah our Lord, through whom we have received grace and apostleship to bring about the obedience of faith for the sake of his name among all the nations, including you [in Rome] who are called to belong to Jesus the Messiah . . . (Romans 1:2-6).[1]

Paul wrote these words to people in Rome! Under Caesar's nose he's announcing another *euangelion*, another piece of "late breaking news" that all those titles Caesar claims for himself, and all his authority, rightfully belong to another Man. They belong to Jesus, the Messiah or anointed one of Israel. Caesar, and all other authorities claiming human allegiance and devotion, are hollow counterfeits of the true Lord.

And, a few lines further, Paul asserts that he's not shy about this gospel. He won't draw back from proclaiming this rival *euangelion*: "I am not ashamed of the gospel, for it is the power of God for salvation to everyone who believes, to the Jew first and also to the Greek" (Romans 1:16), that is, the Gentiles.

---

[1] Scripture quotations in this book are from the English Standard Version. When we quote a New Testament passage that uses the term *Christ* we're substituting the term *Messiah*. Speaking of "Jesus Christ" conveys the impression that Christ was Jesus' last name — as though his parents were Joseph and Mary Christ. That's not what the title means. *Christos* in Greek is equivalent to Hebrew *mashiach*, meaning God's anointed one and the redeemer of Israel. When the New Testament writers, probably all Jewish, use this title for Jesus that's the meaning they intend to convey.

The gospel is the announcement that Jesus is Lord.

The proclamation of *the authority of Jesus over all things* is the gospel of the New Testament. What Paul wrote to the churches of Rome isn't an isolated instance. Think of the defense Paul presented to the assembled bigwigs of Athens, in his famous trial on the Areopagus:

> The times of ignorance God overlooked, but now he commands all people everywhere to repent, because he has fixed a day on which he will judge the world in righteousness by a man whom he has appointed; and of this he has given assurance to all by raising him from the dead (Acts 17:30-31).

Because Jesus has been raised from the dead, Paul is saying, we know that he, and he alone, is the one who will bring justice to this world. *God has appointed Jesus to set things right* — not this local judiciary, and not Caesar or some other so-called divinity.

Obviously such a *euangelion* didn't sit well with people who had a vested interest in the "gospel" of Caesar, or of any other entity claiming worship and devotion. When Paul and Silas announced the news of Jesus at Thessalonica, some members of the local Jewish congregation acknowledged him as Messiah. This upset their leaders; they brought these new Jesus-followers before the local authorities, claiming, "These men who have turned the world upside down have come here also, and Jason [in whose home they met] has received them, and they are all acting against the decrees of Caesar, saying that there is another king, Jesus" (Acts 17:6-7).

Truly, the "breaking news" of Jesus' resurrection, and of his authority as Messiah, was news that "turned the world upside down." The believers' accusers of Thessalonica disliked this message, but they got it right: there is indeed "another king, Jesus," who puts Caesar in his place.

Why would the Jewish leaders of Thessalonica not be glad of such a message? After all, the Jewish homeland was under Roman domination, a regime the Judeans deeply resented. But the Romans had made a special provision for the Jews because of their adamant profession of monotheism. People of other ethnic groups had no problem with worshiping multiple divinities, but for the Jew whose creed was "The LORD our God is one LORD" (Deuteronomy 6:4) this was impossible. So, to keep the peace, the pragmatic Romans excused the Jews from sacrificing *to* Caesar; instead, they simply had to offer temple sacrifices *in Caesar's behalf*. The *status quo* was working for the Jews scattered throughout the Roman Empire; why upset the applecart with a message that the Jewish Messiah has come and is claiming the same allegiance demanded by Caesar? That would make all Jews look like rebels in Roman eyes! And Rome knew how to deal with rebels.

The gospel is a Jewish message.

But the gospel, the *euangelion*, of Paul and other Christian missionaries was a thoroughly Jewish message because it proclaimed Jesus as God's Messiah, his *mashiach* or "anointed one" who has come to rescue and redeem his people Israel. This is evident in the first public announcement of the gospel after the crucifixion of Jesus. On the Day of Pentecost, Peter addressed the Jewish community of Jerusalem with this announcement:

> This Jesus God raised up, and of that we all are witnesses. . . . Let all the house of Israel therefore know for certain that God has made him both Lord and Messiah, this Jesus whom you crucified (Acts 2:32, 36).

The gospel is the "breaking news" of Jesus' resurrection, which makes it evident who he is, after all: the Mes-

siah of Israel and therefore the ruler over all the earth. As
we read in Psalm 2:

> "As for me [God says], I have set my King on Zion,
> my holy hill." I will tell of the decree: The LORD
> said to me, "You are my Son; today I have begot-
> ten you. Ask of me, and I will make the nations
> your heritage, and the ends of the earth your pos-
> session" (Psalm 2:6-8).

It's by virtue of his role as Messiah of Israel that the risen
Jesus can declare to his followers, "All authority in heaven
and on earth has been given to me" (Matthew 28:18).

The Revelation to John is filled with utterances of this
gospel. It begins by announcing "Jesus the Messiah, the
faithful witness, the firstborn of the dead, and the ruler
of kings on earth" (Revelation 1:5). It rises to climactic
pronouncements of the *euangelion:* "The kingdom of the
world has become the kingdom of our Lord and of his
Messiah, and he shall reign forever and ever" (11:15). Such
a message indeed "turns the world upside down" when
it's put forth as the good news, the "breaking news" that
makes a difference, and is acted upon by those who receive it.

Jesus' followers didn't invent this gospel of Jesus'
world-changing appearance. It's a direct development
from the "gospel of God" (Mark 1:14) that Jesus proclaimed in his first public preaching: "The time is fulfilled, and the kingdom of God is at hand; repent, and
believe in the gospel" (Mark 1:15). The Lord, after a long
period when he seemed not to be present to his people,
has now returned to Israel.

There's no mistaking the fact that Jesus saw himself as
the instigator of God's return and the renewal of his kingly
rule. To understand this we have only to review the words
he quoted from the scroll of the prophet Isaiah in the syna-
gogue of Nazareth, his hometown, at the same time:

The Spirit of the Lord is upon me, because he has anointed me to proclaim good news to the poor. He has sent me to proclaim liberty to the captives and recovering of sight to the blind, to set at liberty those who are oppressed, to proclaim the year of the Lord's favor (Luke 4:18-19; Isaiah 61:1-2).

God is on the move once again, Jesus declares, and as his next remark makes clear he sees himself as the one through whom God's return is being realized: "Today this Scripture has been fulfilled in your hearing." The four Gospels of the New Testament are unanimous in their testimony that Jesus exercised the authority of the God of Israel in his teaching, his healing, his extraordinary deeds, and his refutation of those who opposed his work — such that, following the resurrection, his disciples could point out that what he did for his people was public knowledge. You all know, Peter says, "how God anointed Jesus of Nazareth with the Holy Spirit and with power. He went about doing good and healing all who were oppressed by the devil, for God was with him" (Acts 10:38).

The Messiah, the Son of God, is still exercising this authority through his Spirit at work in the world. (See the Appendix for a discussion of how we can visualize this.) As Paul notes, "the Lord is the Spirit" (2 Corinthians 3:17); there's no functional difference between the activity of the risen Jesus and what we call the Holy Spirit. The gospel affirms this ongoing operation of Jesus' authority in both "heaven" ("God's space") and earth (our space), blending them together.

Can you hear the Roman newscaster? "This just in — late breaking news from Judea! Jesus of Nazareth, recently executed for treason, has come back to life and claims to be the Jewish Messiah. He's also claiming the right to govern everything, including this Empire! We have this report from Jerusalem . . ."

If the "late breaking news" of who Jesus is, and the difference he makes in world history, was hidden from anyone while he walked the dusty paths of Galilee and Judea, it was fully revealed by the resurrection which validated his identity as the Messiah of Israel — and therefore the one who has all authority in heaven and earth. That is the *euangelion*, the gospel of the New Testament.

Chapter 2
Whatever Happened to the Gospel?

We have seen that the "breaking news" of Jesus' resurrection, and his authority over all things, is the *euangelion* or gospel of his followers, who spread the message throughout the Roman world and beyond and whose witness is recorded in the New Testament writings. But where is *that* gospel today? How many preachers have you heard who've presented this "late breaking news" as the heart of their message?

The apostle Paul warned the believers of Galatia not to fall for "another gospel," a message different from the one he was proclaiming throughout his extensive travels (Galatians 1:6-9). The Messiah, he said, has come "to deliver us from the present evil age" (Galatians 1:4) with its false values and oppressive structures. In the same vein the apostle John would remind his readers, "The reason the Son of God appeared was to destroy the works of the devil" (1 John 3:8). But it's a temptation to downplay the news of Jesus' resurrection, his victory over the dark powers, and his authority over all things, and to emphasize other concerns which, though often following from that *euangelion*, are not the whole gospel. When this occurs, it's "another gospel" that's being put forward.

"Another gospel" distorts the New Testament's message.

It's true, for example, that forgiveness of sin and reconciliation with God are the consequences of receiving the "breaking news" of Jesus' supremacy. It's also true that better relationships and more successful conduct of life follow from getting in sync with that announcement. But emphasizing these benefits — and pitching the preacher's message toward them — takes the focus off God's victory in the Messiah and places it on the believer and his need. In other words, this "gospel" is all about *me* and not about Jesus. It starts with *me* — how *I* feel, what *I* think of *myself*, what *I* believe *I* need to make *my* life what *I* want it to be. This "gospel" becomes *God's response to my problem*, instead of the announcement that God has done something to change this world — and I'm invited to get on board with this new reality!

Another common "gospel" pitch is the appeal to our awareness of how transient human life is on this earth. People want to believe their lives count for more than whatever can be gained from eking out the traditional "threescore and ten," filled as it often is with suffering and disappointment.[1] (Actually, the Bible says we're allotted 120 years — see Genesis 6:3 — but few people seem to know or want that!) So the "gospel" is offered as a transaction through which we can escape the oppressive finality of death: "Accept Jesus as your Savior, and you'll go to heaven when you die."

---

[1] The seventy-to-eighty-year lifespan is mentioned in Psalm 90, a Psalm of Moses (90:10). It's not a promise but a curse upon the rebellious nation in the wilderness that would never live to see the land of Canaan, the land the Lord had promised them. It should not be taken as the norm for human longevity; that norm is stated in Genesis 6:3.

Yes, the New Testament affirms that in his resurrection Jesus has defeated death, called "the last enemy," and that all who enter into the victorious Messiah take part in his resurrection life, God's new creation. (Spelling that out here would take many pages.) But the "late breaking news" of the *euangelion* never offers our going to heaven as *the purpose* for which Jesus has been given "all authority in heaven and earth."

Instead, the vision of God's triumph in his Messiah is directed toward *the renewal of a just creation*, free from pain and the sorrow of death. As Peter says, "we are waiting for new heavens and a new earth in which righteousness dwells" (2 Peter 3:13). That's where the whole Bible is headed: toward the new creation described on its final pages (Revelation 21:1-5), in which God dwells with his people and all things are made new. We don't have to go to heaven because God is bringing heaven to earth, merging "his space" with our space.

The gospel addresses a community, not just individuals.

This point brings up another aspect of modern "gospel" preaching that contrasts with the New Testament's news about the authority of God's risen Messiah. Today's "gospel" is pitched toward individuals, while the Bible's *euangelion* is *an announcement to a community and a culture.* Religion, in the ancient world, wasn't a private matter. Reverence for the local divinities, and for the "lord" Caesar himself, were public duties expected of all citizens, for that's what religion is: a bond or *ligament* that holds a culture together. The "breaking news" that there's "another king, Jesus," isn't directed toward individuals but toward a community and the culture it embodies. The announcement of Jesus' resurrection threatens the hold that false, lifeless divinities have on people subjected to their regime. It offers freedom to people held in the grip of a dictatorial state, or of any other system that demands religious obedience.

We see this in the first public announcement of Jesus' resurrection, on the Day of Pentecost. After Peter's declaration that his resurrection verifies Jesus' role as Israel's Messiah, his appeal to his Jewish hearers is this: "Save yourselves from this crooked generation" (Acts 2:40). It's not just his hearers' individual sins that have blocked their acceptance of the Messiah, thus barring them from taking part in the new reality God has inaugurated. It's *their culture's sin*, its blindness or indifference to God's long-term plan for his people, that has trapped them. But they can be freed from this enslavement by becoming part of a new community formed around the risen Lord Jesus. And so can non-Jews, likewise trapped in the distorted perspectives of their own cultures. As Peter stresses, the promise of this *euangelion* is also "for all who are far off," that is, the Gentiles.

Preachers have been heard to assert that "Jesus would have died for you if you were the only person in the world," or some similar claim. That is not true. The Messiah died to *lift the curse from a people*, the faithful of Israel, so they could at last fulfill their mission to extend the blessing of Abraham to all nations. As Paul writes in Galatians:

> The Messiah redeemed us from the curse of the law by becoming a curse for us [i.e., us Jews] — for it is written, 'Cursed is everyone who is hanged on a tree' — so that in Messiah Jesus the blessing of Abraham might come to the Gentiles, so that we might receive the promised Spirit through faith (Galatians 3:13-14).

Perhaps if you were the only Israelite Jesus might have died for you. But to extract the gospel from its historical setting in the life of ancient Judaism and drop it, with-

out context, into twenty-first century Western individu-
alistic culture does violence to the plain teaching of Scripture, and distorts the larger picture it paints of God's
dealing with his creation and how we're to see ourselves
in that picture.

The Book of Acts records that on the Day of Pentecost three thousand people "repented" — they adopted
a new perspective or worldview (the Greek word is
metanoia, "change of mind"). They separated themselves
from the warped culture that had kept them from see-
ing what God had been up to in the work of Jesus, and
became what we call the church, the assembly (*ekklesia*)
of those who belong to Jesus.

This message of cultural judgment is what's lacking
in any "gospel" that focuses on the individual and his
need. What's also lacking is the corporate aspect of the
"breaking news," for the two ideas go together. The New
Testament doesn't know any believers in Jesus who
aren't part of the church, participating in the life of a
new community that stands apart from the prevailing
culture and calls it into question. When a person acts
upon the *euangelion* announced to him, his response is
to become a member of Jesus whose resurrection life is
embodied in this new community — a community in
which God's new creation, inaugurated in Jesus' resurrection, is lived out. Christians just lived differently from
their unbelieving neighbors, and this difference was their
witness to the truth of the gospel.

Today, believers are often urged to witness to their
faith by sharing with others the change it has made in
their lives, and perhaps leading them to "accept Jesus
as Lord and Savior." In the world of the New Testament it was the existence of the new-creation community, with its shared life of care and compassion, that
was the witness to what God has done. "If anyone is in

the Messiah," Paul wrote, "there is a new creation" (2 Corinthians 5:17). The Greek is, *Ei tis en christo, kaine ktisis*. It doesn't say, as often quoted, "he (i.e. the believer) is a new creation." There's no "he is" in this sentence. It says that when a person joins up with the body of Christ, which is what "in Christ" or "in the Messiah" means in the New Testament, God's new creation exists *for* that person. The Christian believer has been "raised with the Messiah" (Colossians 3:1) because he belongs to the community formed around the Messiah's life. The way that community functions is to be a foretaste of what's to come when God's new creation is realized in its fulness, when "the earth will be filled with the knowledge of the glory of the LORD as the waters cover the sea" (Habakkuk 2:14).

Today's Christianity has little in common with that of the Bible.

It's easy to see, given these considerations, that Christianity as commonly promoted and practiced often bears little or no resemblance to the faith of the Messiah-people of the New Testament — especially when it has been stripped of its Israelite roots and context. How did that ever happen? To understand what happened, we need to lay out some backstory.

The Bible has a positive view of this material world, which the Creator made and called "very good" (Genesis 1:31). The New Testament hope is not for the abandonment of this material world but for its redemption from the corruption of human sin. People made in the likeness of God, as his representatives in the management of this earth, listened to another voice and abandoned their divine vocation — the scenario depicted in the Bible's opening chapters. To begin working back toward his original design the Lord called a special people, the family of Abraham, to take his name before all nations. So we could say the Bible is divided into two parts: the problem (Genesis 1-11) and the solution (Genesis 12 through the rest of Scripture).

When the people God chose to restore his plan for the world misunderstood what their purpose was and proved not up to the task, one Man came forth who took that whole sinful and disappointing history upon himself and bore it to his cross. That Man could only be Israel's Messiah, the anointed ruler and representative of God's special people. Jesus' authority over evil during his career in Galilee and Judea, and then his overcoming of death — sin's ultimate weapon — makes it clear the he is "the man whom God has appointed," the Messiah prefigured in the Hebrew Scriptures who is to govern all things. This very Jewish story now expands into the environment originally intended for it in God's call of Abraham, the context of "every tribe and language and people and nation" (Revelation 5:9). That, of course, is where we come in, as a result of the announcement of the New Testament's "late breaking news" to the whole world.

But after the New Testament period, as the church moved out of its Jewish environment into the pagan world of Greece and Rome, the Israelite context of what Jesus had accomplished became obscured and non-biblical ideas began to infiltrate Christian thought. Plato, the iconic Greek philosopher, drew a distinction between the exalted, timeless realm of ideas and the low, crass world of the time-bound material — a distinction foreign to the Bible's way of thinking. Under the influence of his followers, chiefly the pagan priest and author Plutarch, Christian thinkers began to lose their focus on the *euangelion* of Jesus' authority and its historical sweep over the institutions of this world.

The purpose of uniting with Jesus shifted from "reigning in life" with him (Romans 5:17) to escaping from this material plane into the timeless realm of God's eternity. Jesus' death and resurrection came to be viewed not as the inauguration of God's new creation but as the key to leaving the corrupt space-time universe behind for the delights of heaven. That, of course, is how the Christian "gospel" is still often presented to people. "This world is not my home, I'm only passing through" has sometimes become the motto of the Christian, a sentiment flatly contrary to God's stated purpose in creating mankind: to manage this earth as his representative, to "be fruitful and multiply and fill the earth and subdue it, and have dominion" over what God has made (Genesis 1:28). As Psalm 115 states, "The heavens are the LORD's heavens, but the earth he has given to the children of man" (Psalm 115:16). Instead of confining their faith to "spiritual" matters the Lord's people are to extend their involvement into politics, commerce, the arts, education, technology, and other human enterprises that, for so long, have been handed over to forces indifferent to the purposes of God.

The focus on the individual is "another gospel."

Other influences besides the philosophy of Plato and his followers played their part in muting the gospel's "late breaking news." A major factor was the rise of the ideology of Gnosticism. The Greek word *gnosis* means "knowledge," in this case an esoteric knowledge attainable only by the select few, a kind of internal self-discovery. Such a special knowledge raises its adherents above the level of ordinary, ignorant people. Jesus came to be regarded as the dispenser of this secret knowledge, even to the extent that his actual deeds, including his death and resurrection, dropped out of his portrait in Gnostic books like the Gospel of Thomas.

The wider church condemned this movement of "what is falsely called knowledge" (1 Timothy 6:20) as a heresy, a dangerously misleading teaching, and held to the four Gospels we know from the New Testament. But the damage was done, and to this day some present the Christian faith as a matter of getting in touch with our deepest self where, above all, the believer can connect with Jesus. Others reject the believer's involvement with the institutions of the prevailing culture, insisting that separation from the "world" means staying clear of politics or other public arenas and focusing exclusively on one's personal "spirituality." Still others insist that Christian faith is a matter of having the correct knowledge of Christian doctrine, and if you don't agree with their teaching or their particular interpretation of the Bible you aren't really a Christian.

What marked these distortions, and others like them, was not only the de-emphasis on the *euangelion*, the announcement that Jesus alone is Lord, but also the focus on the individual believer instead of the community of faith. It's not just to know the truth, but to "follow the truth" (3 John 1) by practicing a way of life, that marks the New Testament Christian. And *that way of life is worked out in community* with other members of the body of the Messiah. The risen Jesus commissioned his followers not only to make disciples by baptizing people into Jesus, but also to teach them to observe the way of life he set forth for them. Paul summarizes that way when he says, "Bear one another's burdens, and so fulfill the law of Christ" (Galatians 6:2). I can't keep this "law" by myself; to minister to "one another" I have to be involved in the common life of the new community formed around the resurrection life of Jesus.

Regrettably, in our Western culture few local groups we call churches are realizing this New Testament vision for the common life of God's new creation, which

Jesus released into this world by his resurrection. Most churches function like religious clubs or stage productions, pitching their participation or membership appeal in a manner that treats people like consumers of a product or spectators being entertained. In this situation it's no wonder people hop from church to church looking for the "biggest bang for their buck" because what counts is *how effectively I perceive my needs to be met.*

What if Christian congregations viewed themselves as a family, as did the New Testament community, and conducted their life in a family-like manner — "bearing one another's burdens"? Would there be less of a tendency to think of ourselves as consumers of a religious product, shopping around for the best deal? Perhaps because family ties themselves have become less meaningful in our culture, we've downplayed the New Testament emphasis on the family-like nature of the Christian congregation in which members conduct themselves not as isolated, self-centered individuals but as brothers and sisters involved in helping each other realize the benefits of living in God's new creation. As the Letter to the Hebrews expresses this ideal, "Let us consider how to stir up one another to love and good works, not neglecting to meet together, as is the habit of some, but encouraging one another" (Hebrews 10:24-25).

Scientific materialism forced the gospel into retreat.

We've discussed several factors that have transformed the New Testament's "breaking news" of Jesus' resurrection and his authority over all things into "another gospel." The New Testament's *euangelion* is the announcement of God's long-range plan for the transformation of this world, but the "gospel" often heard today is focused instead on people's personal needs or their hope to escape this world, at death, into a timeless eternity. But we must discuss another major cause for this evolution into "another gospel."

In the eighteenth century in Western civilization a movement emerged known as the Enlightenment, a movement characterized by scientific materialism. In this philosophy, or worldview, the only real world is the natural, or physical, world that can be studied by the instruments of science and by direct observation. Anything "supernatural," or not detectable or verifiable by scientific methods, is ruled out of consideration.

The roots of scientific materialism can be traced to the ancient philosophy of Epicureanism, popularized by the Roman poet Lucretius in his first-century-BC work *De Rerum Natura* which attributed all natural phenomena to the random collision of atoms falling through space. With the emergence of scientific materialism the Bible, with its record of interaction with an invisible God and its accounts of seemingly miraculous happenings, came to be viewed as the work of primitive, gullible, and unenlightened minds who invented stories of events that never could have occurred.

Although many prominent figures contributed to the rise of scientific materialism, an influential spokesman and popularizer of this worldview was the Scottish philosopher David Hume. Since, in his ethnically limited British Isles environment, he had never encountered a supernatural or miraculous event, he concluded that his was the universal experience of all enlightened humanity. Reports of such events, instead of being taken seriously and investigated, must simply be ruled out of court at the outset. In other words Hume's reasoning, supposedly logical, violated the rules of logic by including his intended conclusion in the evidence meant to bolster that conclusion.

Hume's logical error escaped his notice and the notice of all who adopted the philosophy of scientific materialism, and has continued to infect much scientific and popular discussion to this day. For example, biological evidence that calls into question the theory of unguided evolution — such as the discovery that the DNA of all living organisms is a sequential information code implying an originating intelligence — must be rejected because evolution is held to be such an established fact that no evidence against it may be admitted. It's easy to see that scientific materialism, rather than being a scientific approach to reality, is actually a doctrine held with religious fervor by its faithful adherents.

But this Enlightenment worldview came to pervade Western culture to the point that the gospel's "breaking news" of Jesus' resurrection and headship over all things was shoved into a spiritual compartment removed from the "real world" of earthly life. God and all issues relating to his existence and activity were relegated to an invisible realm irrelevant to the space-time universe in which we live.

Sadly, the church went along with this move. Christian leaders, believing they had no defense against scientific materialism, surrendered the realm of the natural world to the physical sciences and retreated into a spiritual ghetto where the invisible realities of the faith couldn't be touched by science. The historical and corporate impact of the "breaking news" of the *euangelion* was lost to view. Religion became a personal matter instead of a public concern. Under the worldview of scientific materialism the "gospel" became the offer of an invisible, internal transaction between the individual and God that promised escape from the space-time universe into a timeless eternity upon the believer's death. And that scenario is still playing itself out in most Christian circles.

The gospel is coming into its own.

Nevertheless, a change is in the air. Science itself has shattered the complacency of Hume's scientific materialism. The universe, far from being easily explained by the steady accumulation of data, turns out be a far more mysterious place than was assumed. No longer seen as eternally existent, the universe — not only material substance but space and time themselves — are now understood to have begun in a singular event commonly, though erroneously, called the "big bang."

Time is no longer regarded as a constant, but as malleable in relation to acceleration toward the speed of light. The tight galactic perspective of former decades has become an ever-expanding universe of uncounted billions of galaxies. Space itself can be warped, in a manner no one really understands, and gravity is not a force but the effect of this distortion. It's claimed that ninety-five percent or more of the universe consists of "dark" matter and energy, not detectable by electromagnetic media (such as light or radio waves) but inferred only from their effects on gravity and the expansion of the universe.

We've already mentioned the presence of digital information, which statistically could never have arisen merely from chance and the passage of time, in the nuclei of living cells. The very nature of hard reality itself is called into question by the finding that, at the subatomic scale, immense distances separate the particles of matter so that even what appears to be solid is mostly space. As for the particles themselves, theories are proposed that even the subatomic entities identified by physicists (quarks, mesons, gluons and the like) are not "stuff" but simply frequencies vibrating across multiple dimensions.

Moreover the resurrection of Jesus, far from being the later fabrication of hopeful followers ignorant of the finality of death, has been shown to be the core of Christian proclamation within a few short years of Jesus' crucifixion. Historical inquiry has exposed the false assumption that the Gospel accounts could have been invented decades after the events they record; they can be explained only as arising from eyewitness accounts of something quite unexpected but nevertheless occurring in the arena of human history.[2] The "late breaking news" is news once again.

Whatever happened to the gospel? Under the sway of Platonic philosophy, Gnosticism, individualism, and scientific materialism the New Testament's true message has been replaced by "another gospel." In the face of world cultures going berserk with irrationality, violence, and injustice of all sorts, that "other gospel" has collapsed into irrelevance. The "old, old story" that some people love to sing about — but which isn't the New Testament's real story — has lapsed into a repetitive mantra that grips the attention of fewer people with each passing year.

But the *euangelion* of the New Testament, the announcement of Jesus' resurrection and his world-changing authority, is what the apostle Paul called "the power of God for salvation," a force that delivers people from the shackles of false ideologies and regimes that mar the image in which God created them. Long suppressed by fake news, the "late breaking news" of the Bible has gone into eclipse. It's high time to bring it back.

---

[2] For an exhaustive treatment of this evidence see N. T. Wright, *The Resurrection of the Son of God* (Fortress, 2003).

Chapter 3
God's Treaty With Us

The gospel of the New Testament proclaims the risen Jesus to be Lord, Savior, and Son of God — titles claimed by Caesar. But it wasn't in response to the Roman emperor that Jesus was hailed in this manner. It was in response to themes already present in the Hebrew Scriptures — what we call the Old Testament — that Jesus, having been raised from the dead by the power of God, was now understood to be the exalted ruler of all. The word "Lord" (*kurios*) was how the Greek Old Testament rendered the divine name of God, *Yahweh*, in the Hebrew text; among Greek-speaking Jewish followers of the Messiah, like the apostle Paul and the writers of the Gospels, this title came ready to hand as a title for the risen Jesus, the Son of God.

What some Christian teachers forget, or fail to stress, is that the early church had no Scriptures except the books of the Hebrew Bible, in Greek translation. It was in those writings that the apostles, and those who followed them into the faith of the Messiah, found the clues to what the resurrection of Jesus meant for the world. The risen Jesus explained to his followers, "Everything written about me in the Law of Moses and the Prophets and the Psalms must be fulfilled" (Luke 24:44).

And Paul, writing to the Corinthian church, related what he had been given as the earliest Christian teaching: "For I delivered to you as of first importance what I also received: that the Messiah died for our sins in accordance with the Scriptures, that he was buried, that he was raised on the third day in accordance with the Scriptures" (1 Corinthians 15:3-4).

Many Jews of the first century believed in the resurrection of the nation of Israel as a corporate entity; as an instance, the prophet Ezekiel's vision of the dry bones coming to life (Ezekiel 37:1-14) expresses this hope. But no one expected that one Man would be raised as the precursor to that resurrection. The startling events that followed closely upon Jesus' crucifixion forced his disciples to comb the Scriptures for indications that the rise of their Messiah had been foreseen. Their conclusion was that his resurrection was the fulfillment of what God had planned all along in commissioning Israel — beginning with Abraham, Genesis 12:2-3, 18:17-18 — to make his name and his blessing known to all peoples.

What the nation as a whole had failed to do its Messiah had now done, fulfilling in himself the purposes for which God had called a people to serve him. Thus, as Peter stated on the Day of Pentecost, the promise is not only for the Jews but also "for all who are far off" (Acts 2:39). The universal and just rule of Israel's Messiah was an established hope in the Hebrew Scriptures, expressed in the Psalms (as we have noted) and elsewhere. Through the resurrection of Jesus it had now been inaugurated in the earth. There is, indeed, "another King, Jesus," whose authority supersedes that of Caesar or any other entity or ideology with a counterfeit claim to human devotion and obedience.

The Lordship of Jesus is effected through his covenant.

A king, or lord, has authority over those in his realm. But how does a king exercise his governance? Kings are less common in our world than they used to be, and many of those remaining are kings or queens in name only, their role restricted to a few ceremonial functions. Nevertheless we're familiar with dictatorial regimes, like that of North Korea or the Islamic state of Iran, that demand total conformity and obedience and enforce their rule by oppressive measures.

As Jesus pointed out to his disciples, "You know that the rulers of the Gentiles lord it over them, and their great ones exercise authority over them" (Matthew 20:25). But he went on to give them a different model for the exercise of authority in his name: the model of servanthood and self-giving to the fellow members of their community.

Jesus' words highlight the responsibility his followers have to one another under his headship. If that's the case, there must be a relationship structure within which his authority, as Lord and Son of God, is put into effect and worked out. It would be a relationship of mutual responsibility, each party having his role to play. The apostle John hints at this when he writes, "We love because he first loved us" (1 John 4:19), and then points out that God's love for us calls upon us to extend that same love, or commitment (*agape*), to other members of his family.

Jesus didn't invent this relationship of mutual obligation; it's the foundational thrust of the Scriptures he commended to his disciples and to us. The name the Bible gives this structure is the *covenant*, the agreement God makes with his human partners. This agreement is summarized in several places in both the Old and New Testaments. A brief but clear statement of the covenant appears, for example, in the prophecy of Jeremiah: "I will be their God, and they shall be my people" (Jeremiah 31:33). It's restated at the very end of the Bible, in John's vision of the emerging new creation: "Behold, the dwelling place of God is with man. He will dwell with them, and they will be his people, and God himself will be with them as their God" (Revelation 21:3).

These concise statements imply the responsibilities of both partners to the agreement. God is to be *God*, doing what God is supposed to do for his people: protecting them, directing them, and providing for them. And the people are to be *his* people, not someone else's; they're to be his loyal servants and willingly follow that way of life he lays out for them. If this covenant gets turned around so that God becomes the servant, answering to our beck and call as we put ourselves in the driver's seat, then we're no longer exercising biblical faith.

As an instance, when an event occurs that causes serious human suffering — a tsunami, an earthquake, a terrorist attack, a school shooting — people ask, "Where was God?" The atheist asks in scorn, while the believer asks in regret. But the question implies that God's duty is to serve the needs of humanity; if something evil occurs, either God doesn't exist or he's failed to live up to his responsibilities. The gospel, in contrast, announces that God, through his Son, has "all authority in heaven and earth" and calls on all creation to obey him and *serve his purpose*. To ask, "Where was God?" is like the tail wagging the dog. It seems an odd thing, after all, that people would assume that the reality, or the goodness, of the Creator of a universe of billions of galaxies should depend on what occurs to one or more individuals on a small planet hidden in an arm of the Milky Way. God is much "bigger" than that. Nevertheless, God's covenant offers a plan through which, all else being equal, the benefits of his goodness may accrue to his human partners.

God's covenant has a clear structure.

The Bible's structure of the covenant resembles the structure of ancient Near Eastern treaties between a "great king," or emperor, and the client kings (the Medieval term is *vassals*) who govern under him. In these treaties, which came to light as the result of archaeological findings in the early twentieth century, the great king announces his presence and offers a historical prologue reciting what he has done for his treaty partners. He then lays out the stipulations of the agreement he's making with them. They're to be loyal to no other ruler, only to him; they're to keep and enforce his laws; they're to join him in battle against enemies; and they're to be at peace with one another within his empire.[1]

If the client kings keep faith with the great king they will enjoy the benefits of his benevolent rule. But, lest any be unfaithful to this agreement, the great king lays down sanctions for disobedience in the form of curses bringing all manner of punishments upon them. He then invokes witnesses to this agreement, usually his gods and the gods of his clients. Finally, the parties to the treaty seal it by a rite: a sacrifice, or a ceremonial meal in which the clients take part.

In Scripture the best example of this treaty-covenant structure is the Book of Deuteronomy, a long sermon by Moses as the Israelites are about to cross the River Jordan into Canaan. Moses is conducting a renewal of the

---

[1] The groundbreaking work that brought these treaties to light was Viktor Korošec, *Hethitische Staatsvertäge: Ein Beitrag zu ihrer juristischen Wertung* (Leipzig, 1931). George E. Mendenhall drew out their implications for the understanding of the biblical covenant in his monograph *Law and Covenant in Israel and the Ancient Near East* (Pittsburgh, 1954).

covenant the Lord granted Israel at Mount Sinai, with the Lord appearing in the role of the "great King." After a recital of Israel's progress toward this moment, the Lord declares who he is and what he's done for his people: "I am the LORD [*Yahweh*] your God, who brought you out of the land of Egypt, out of the house of slavery" (Deuteronomy 5:6). The Lord then lays down his treaty stipulation of total loyalty to himself: "You shall have no other gods before me" (5:7). After amplifying the requirements that go along with allegiance to their great King, the Lord states how he requires his treaty partners to behave toward one another with commandments about murder, adultery, theft, false witness, and "coveting" —manipulating others to secure for ourselves what belongs to them (5:17-21).

With this background in the Hebrew Scriptures it's easy to see how Jesus, as risen Lord with all authority, can give his followers a way of life to pursue out of loyalty to him, and command them to instruct others in how to follow it as well —"teaching them to observe all that I have commanded you" (Matthew 28:20). His primary commandment for his followers is, of course, that of mutual commitment and compassion for one another: "A new commandment I give to you, that you love one another: just as I have loved you, you also are to love one another. By this all people will know that you are my disciples, if you have love for one another" (John 13:34-35).

The biblical structure of the covenant, God's treaty with his people, places the risen Son of God in the position of the great King who expects his partners to be loyal to him and to one another. Thus the apostle Paul can speak of "the law of the Messiah" which involves "bearing one another's burdens." The "late breaking news" of the *euangelion* implies that a covenant, or treaty, is being put into place.

God's treaty with us means actions have consequences.

But we're only halfway through the structure of this biblical agreement between God and his people. In ancient treaty structure, once the great king has laid down the requirements he expects of the rulers under him he pronounces the sanctions of the agreement: benefits when his partners remain faithful, but curses upon them should they prove disloyal. In the covenant structure of Deuteronomy the blessings and curses appear in chapter 28.

If God's people faithfully obey him they will be victorious over enemies and will be blessed with prosperity; they will be "the head and not the tail" (Deuteronomy 28:13). If they falter in their loyalty to the Lord they will be subjected to the curses of poverty, disease, defeat, and horrors so unspeakable that we wouldn't care to hear verses 15-68 read aloud! Commitment to the Lord and faithful adherence to the ways he has set forth will have their reward in a life of blessing, but spurning him and his directives will have the opposite effect.

The sanctions of the covenant — the blessings and curses — underscore an established biblical principle that *actions, for good or ill, have consequences*. The principle appears throughout Scripture, not just where the covenant structure is as clear as we find it in Deuteronomy. The Book of Proverbs is based on this theme; wise decisions lead to successful living, but ignoring the way of the Lord leads to ruin. This principle extends to the New Testament as well; we hear Jesus telling us, among other things, that if we seek first to live under God's kingly and righteous rule we'll receive the needs of everyday life (Matthew 6:33). Or we read Paul's admonition that "God is not mocked, for whatever one sows, that will he also reap" (Galatians 6:7).

The nexus of action and consequence applies universally, even beyond the framework of God's covenant with his people. If a person refuses to acknowledge God and adopts a lifestyle contrary to his design for human conduct, he'll experience a serious deterioration in his quality of life. Paul makes this clear in his Letter to the Romans:

> For the wrath of God is revealed from heaven against all ungodliness and unrighteousness of men, who by their unrighteousness suppress the truth. For what can be known about God is plain to them, because God has shown it to them. For his invisible attributes, namely, his eternal power and divine nature, have been clearly perceived, ever since the creation of the world, in the things that have been made. So they are without excuse. For although they knew God, they did not honor him as God or give thanks to him, but they became futile in their thinking, and their foolish hearts were darkened. Claiming to be wise, they became fools, and exchanged the glory of the immortal God for images resembling mortal man and birds and animals and creeping things. Therefore God gave them up in the lusts of their hearts to impurity, to the dishonoring of their bodies among themselves, because they exchanged the truth about God for a lie and worshiped and served the creature rather than the Creator, who is blessed forever! Amen (Romans 1:18-25).

Through creation, Paul insists, everyone should understand that God is real, and acknowledge him (what "giving thanks" means in this context). He goes on to elaborate on the degenerate lifestyle to which people subject themselves when they scorn the truth of God's Word. That lifestyle itself, with the heartache it creates, is the curse of the covenant being put into effect.

So the "late breaking news" of the lordship of Jesus, the great King, brings with it a mandate for a conduct of life that reflects the new creation inaugurated in his resurrection from the dead. This mandate is expressed repeatedly in the New Testament in passages such as Romans 12, where Paul insists that followers of Jesus must take on a different worldview, the renewal of their mind that liberates them from the warped thinking of the prevailing culture. In so doing they're to shun evil; honor and serve one another; share each other's joys and sorrows; exhibit humility; and overcome slights or mistreatment by returning good. Paul's words are a direct echo of how Jesus instructed his followers to act in teachings such as his Sermon on the Mount, Matthew 5–7. Such admonitions are a clear spin-off from the directives found in biblical instances of covenant structure such as Deuteronomy.

Accepting God's offer of partnership in the covenant involves making a decision. Joshua, Moses' successor, laid this decision before Israel in his memorable words, "Choose this day whom you will serve" (Joshua 24:15). Scripture constantly calls us to make, or reaffirm, our decision to be covenant partners with the Lord. Receiving the benefits the great King intends to confer upon his faithful is contingent upon choosing his way of life over whatever tempting, but destructive, course of life we may be led into by our emotions or by cultural pressure.

Were that not the case, the word *if* wouldn't be found so frequently on the pages of Holy Scripture. "All these blessings shall come upon you and overtake you, *if* you obey the voice of the LORD your God" (Deuteronomy 28:2). "*If* my people who are called by my name humble themselves, and pray and seek my face and turn from their wicked ways, then I will hear from heaven and will forgive their sin and heal their land" (2 Chronicles 7:14). "Whatever you ask in prayer, you will receive, *if* you have faith" (Matthew 21:22). "*If* you live according to the flesh [self-centered emotions] you will die, but *if* by the Spirit you put to death the deeds of the body, you will live" (Romans 8:13). "*If* we endure, we will also reign with him; *if* we deny him, he also will deny us" (2 Timothy 2:12).

God's treaty with us is for our benefit.

Remaining in partnership with the risen Lord, then, requires continual reaffirmation of our loyalty to him and the constant exercise of the choices implied by that pesky word *if*. But, lest we suppose the Lord's rescue of us from "the present evil age" depends on our deeds or "works" rather than his love and mercy, we must recall that his very offer of a covenant is an act of grace. As Moses reminded the Israelites, it wasn't because they were anything special or deserved particular favor that the Lord had rescued them from Egyptian slavery but because of his own faithfulness to the promises he'd made to their ancestors. That was the expression of his love, or commitment, to them (Deuteronomy 7:7-8).

It was always God's love — not some harsh, demanding motive on his part — that made the covenant possible. Israel's most perceptive thinkers realized this fundamental truth. "He declares his word to Jacob, his statutes and rules to Israel. He has not dealt thus with any other nation; they do not know his rules. Hallelujah!" (Psalm 147:19-20). Following the way of life set forth in God's Word isn't a matter of earning his favor; it's what Paul called "the obedience of faith"(Romans 16:26) — the loyal, respectful, and grateful honoring of the desires of a gracious Father. God's covenant partners are also his family, and to be one of his family members is what the Bible means by being "righteous," rightly connected to the great King and putting his justice into effect. To be "justified" is to be recognized, by the Lord, as being one of his covenant partners and a member of his family.

The benefits of coming under the headship of the great King are stated in his contract with us. To receive those benefits we don't need to pray and beg the Lord for them. If you have a job, come payday you don't plead with your employer for your paycheck or direct deposit. It will come regularly as long as you're employed and doing your job; it's in your contract. The same applies to God's covenant with us. Through the nexus of act and consequence the benefits he promises will flow into our life as long as we hold up our end of the bargain, and remain loyal members of his family.

Sometimes people say, "You never know what God will do." That's a pagan way of thinking. As biblical worshipers we know exactly what God will do in response to our faithfulness, because we have his word for it. The counsel of the Book of Proverbs is that "the reward for humility and fear of the Lord is riches and honor and life" (Proverbs 22:4).

We've discussed several phases in the way the Lord's agreement with us plays out: His declaration of who he is and what he's done for us; the obligations he lays down for his treaty partners; the sanctions, both for good and ill, that enforce our faithfulness to him based on the life-choices we make. It remains to discuss the final sections of the covenant structure, the invocation of witnesses and the sealing of the agreement.

The treaty includes witness and worship.

In ancient Near Eastern treaties outside Israel, the great king invokes his gods and those of the client kings with whom he's establishing his agreement. For Israel, firmly committed to its creed that "The LORD our God is one LORD," false gods could never be invoked as witnesses. In their place, in our example from Deuteronomy, Moses calls upon other witnesses to put their stamp on the agreement, just as today witnesses sign a will to validate the testator's signature. "I call heaven and earth to witness against you today, that I have set before you life and death, blessing and curse. Therefore choose life, that you and your offspring may live" (Deuteronomy 30:19). Other passages express the same thought: "He calls to the heavens above and to the earth, that he may judge his people" (Psalm 50:4).

God's own creation — "heaven and earth," Genesis 1:1 — is summoned to monitor the covenant he makes with his partners. If "the things that have been made" testify to the reality of their Creator (Romans 1:29), they also testify to the choice people make to enter into partnership with their great King. When, in the Revelation to John, the apostle sees "a new heaven and a new earth" he's not speaking of the replacement of the physical universe by another material entity. He's speaking of *the renewal and fulfillment of the covenant* in God's new creation, for which the witnesses must be newly invoked.[2]

The treaty must then be sealed by a ceremony. It may be a sacrifice, and the New Testament refers in several places to Jesus' sacrifice of his own life to institute the covenant. "The Messiah loved us and gave himself up for us, a fragrant offering and sacrifice to God" (Ephesians 5:2). But along with the sacrifice, the shedding of blood, there's a ceremonial meal shared by the participants in the agreement.

---

[2] The Revelation to John is all about covenant: its violation by the unfaithful city, the curse that must then fall upon that city and what it represents, and the renewal of the covenant with those who've bonded with God's Messiah to become his new family, the community Paul calls "the Israel of God" (Galatians 6:16).

These elements aren't present in Deuteronomy, but we find them in the account of the covenant on Mount Sinai. After receiving the commandments Moses reads the Book of the Covenant to the people. When they pledge their loyalty to the Lord's commands they reply, "All that the LORD has spoken we will do, and we will be obedient." Then Moses sprinkles the sacrificial blood upon the people declaring, "Behold the blood of the covenant that the LORD has made with you in accordance with all these words" (Exodus 24:7-8). He then takes the leaders of the people up the mountain for the meal in God's presence that further seals the agreement: "they beheld God, and ate and drank" (Exodus 24:11).

The Book of Deuteronomy, with its treaty structure, records Moses leading a ceremony of the renewal of God's covenant with his people. This ceremony is an act of worship. Christian worship today, to be biblically informed, needs to be shaped and enacted as a renewal of the covenant. Virtually all the elements are there, or ought to be: the vision of God's greatness, the declaration of his acts that have delivered us from bondage to false authorities, the proclamation of the Word of instruction in the Lord's way of life, and the pronouncement of blessing upon those who go forth to live that life in faithfulness.

And, finally, there's the meal that seals the agreement, the meal we call the Lord's Supper or Holy Communion. Like the leaders of Israel on Mount Sinai, in gathering at the Lord's Table we "behold God and eat and drink." This rite isn't just a visual aid to help us remember the death of Jesus; it's also a participation in his resurrection life, as lived out in the community gathered in his name. Paul asks,

> The cup of blessing that we bless, is it not a participation [*koinonia*, common life] in the blood of the Messiah? The bread that we break, is it not a participa-

tion in the body of the Messiah? Because there is one bread, we who are many are one body, for we all partake of the one bread (1 Corinthians 10:16-17).

The ceremony of the Lord's Table is the reenactment of the bond that unites Christian worshipers as treaty partners with the Lord and with one another. As Jesus stated in instituting this rite, "This is my blood of the covenant, which is poured out for many" (Mark 14:24).

Sometimes Christian teachers downplay the ritual or ceremonial aspect of worship in favor of understanding worship as continual inward fellowship with the Lord and devotion to him in all areas of life. It's true that performing a mindless ritual while lacking a heartfelt bond with the Lord, or a commitment to obey him, earns the condemnation of both the Israelite prophets (e.g., Isaiah 1:12-13; Amos 5:21-24) and Jesus himself (Matthew 15:7-9, quoting Isaiah 29:13). Nevertheless a concept of worship lacking specific actions can be a nebulous idea, of no help at all to a believer wanting to grow in the faith. Scripture is specific about what worship is: the *visible* expression of humility before the great King and submission to his rule under the covenant.

The biblical words translated "worship" make this clear. The Hebrew word *hishtachavah* signifies falling prostrate before a higher authority, and the Greek word *proskuneo* describes kneeling or prostration. When the disciples met the risen Jesus, they "took hold of his feet and worshiped him" (Matthew 28:9). In John's vision of worship before God's throne the elders and living creatures "fell down and worshiped God" (Revelation 19:4).

Movement, gestures, and specific actions such as participating in the Lord's Supper, even if we call them "ritual," are mandated as the expression of homage and commitment to the Lord. They're part of the tribute the treaty partners of the great King bring before him. In-

ternalizing the concept of worship into something occurring "in the heart" alone allows a person to claim to
be a worshiper while giving his fellow members in the
family of God no clear evidence of his commitment.

What's missing in the foregoing description of Christian worship, as a renewal of the biblical covenant? The
curses, the fearful consequence of unfaithfulness to the
Lord, aren't present. Jesus has taken that sanction upon
himself in order to release his people from them. Paul
wrote to the Galatian believers, "The Messiah redeemed
us from the curse of the law by becoming a curse for us"
(Galatians 3:13).[3]

The ultimate curse is, of course, death, but in the resurrection of the Son of God death has been defeated.
Paul reminds the Roman believers that when a person
is baptized into the Messiah he dies with him and is
raised with him into new life (Romans 6:3-4). "He who
is joined to the Lord becomes one spirit with him" (1
Corinthians 6:17), so that if a person is in the Messiah
he's participating in the new-creation life Jesus brought
into the world. This is clear New Testament teaching;
it's the outcome of the *euangelion*, the announcement that
the risen Jesus is the Son of God and therefore the Lord,
or final authority, over all things.

---

[3] It's not the law, the *Torah* of Moses, that is the curse
from which Jesus has released us; as Paul wrote to the
Romans, "The law is holy, and the commandment is
holy and righteous and good" (Romans 7:12). The Torah lays out the curse (Deuteronomy 28) but it also lays
out a way to avoid it. Because of sin, however, that way
was not followed.

Chapter 4
The Good News of Health and Prosperity

The "late breaking news" of Jesus' resurrection and his authority over all things carries with it the declaration of the covenant the Lord makes with his partners on the human scene. The Bible's covenant structure, as we've seen in Deuteronomy and elsewhere, depicts the Lord in the position of the great King entering into agreement with his servants, or partners. By analogy with ancient Near Eastern treaties that were part of the Bible's cultural background, Jesus' relation to his followers is like that of an emperor to his client rulers. But lest we imagine that such an arrangement demeans us as mere servants or slavish sycophants, notice this: *a king doesn't make a treaty with peons.* A king makes a treaty with *other kings*, with people who have an authority of their own!

God's treaty with us is intended to reestablish our calling as people made in his image, entrusted with the management of our world and prepared to "reign in life" through membership in Messiah Jesus. As Jesus told his disciples in the upper room, "No longer do I call you servants, for the servant does not know what his master is doing; but I have called you friends" (John 15:15). The covenant elevates the Lord's partners to a status comparable, within their own sphere of activity, to his status in the wider universe so that, as Peter says, we become "par-

takers of the divine nature" (2 Peter 1:4). Echoing the declaration of Genesis that "God created man in his own
image" (Genesis 1:27) the hymn of Psalm 8 states, "You
have made him a little lower than the heavenly beings
and crowned him with glory and honor. You have given
him dominion over the works of your hands" (Psalm 8:5-
6). Where this exalted human vocation has been suppressed and distorted by powers opposed to the Creator's
intent, the covenant — the treaty of the great King —
restores it.

God's covenant gives us authority in the world.

The calling of those who belong to Jesus is to function as the hymn in the Revelation to John portrays them:
"You have made them a kingdom and priests to our God,
and they shall reign on the earth" (Revelation 5:10). In
the new community centered in the risen Messiah, John
sees the fulfillment of the Lord's declaration to Israel in
the covenant on Mount Sinai: "You shall be to me a kingdom of priests and a holy nation" (Exodus 19:6). Members of Jesus' new creation perform the priestly functions of worship and prayer in the Lord's presence, and
also exercise kingly authority over whatever situations
in their life and environment threaten deprivation, illness, dysfunctional relationships, or anything that rises
up against God's will for his people.

In the ancient treaty the client kings receive their authority only as they submit to the rule of the great king.
As followers of Jesus we're able to exercise our dominion over the circumstances of life, so that we're never
"under the circumstances," to the extent that we're in
compliance with the requirements of his agreement with
us. As a Roman centurion recognized — and Jesus commended him as an example of faith (Mark 8:8-10) —
only those who are *under* authority *have* authority.[1] That

being established, as "one spirit with the Lord" believers share the purpose for which the Lord Jesus was manifested in the world, "to destroy the works of the devil" (1 John 3:8). Jesus told his audience, "The thief [the enemy of God's work] comes only to steal and kill and destroy. I came that they may have life and have it abundantly" (John 10:10). That abundant life, Scripture makes clear, is the outcome of faithfulness to the pattern of life our great King offers us in his treaty.

The "other gospel's" over-spiritualization and internalization of the New Testament's *euangelion* has muted the force of this contract. It has resulted in Christians' begging or pleading with God for things he has already declared belong to us if we uphold our part of the bargain and "seek first his kingdom and his righteousness." It has caused believers to abdicate their responsibility to influence and direct the course of historical events and, instead, to seek escape into a spiritual ghetto and, ultimately, into an immaterial heaven. The "other gospel" is an accommodation to the schemes of the hideous power that would "steal and kill and destroy," for it reduces people to helpless peons of a capricious overlord reluctant to dispense his favors in this life.

Moreover, this "other gospel," influenced by Platonic and Gnostic contempt for the material world, has elevated the curses of sickness and poverty to the status of virtues. Sometimes it is said that God uses illness or financial lack to test us, or to teach his people some truth about their lives, or to refine them in their walk of faith. The glorification of poverty, for example,

---

[1] Hence Paul's sarcastic remarks about Christians in the troubled Corinthian congregation who attempted to assume the authority of "kings" while disregarding the moral and ethical requirements of the covenant (1 Corinthians 4:8).

has infected Christian thinking to the point that Roman Catholic priests or members of religious orders take a vow of poverty.

In the early 1200s Francesco Bernardone, a well-to-do young man from Assisi in Italy, forsook his wealth and adopted a lifestyle of poverty, becoming known as St. Francis and a paradigm for the pathway to sainthood through forsaking earthly goods. Francis was following a long-established tradition in the church that viewed poverty as a more godly state than the enjoyment of the bounty of God's creation. In the fifth century AD a man named Simeon, from the Roman province of Cilicia, lived for thirty-seven years on a small platform atop a pillar that eventually reached a height of fifty feet; for his ascetic lifestyle he became revered as St. Simeon Stylites.

Jesus and the early Christians didn't model poverty.

Disdain for the covenant benefits of health, prosperity, and successful living can be traced in part to a false view of the life of Jesus and his followers in the New Testament record. Jesus is depicted as a poor and simple workman and his disciples as unschooled peasants or fishermen lacking the resources for prosperous living. But another picture emerges when we remove the filter of the "sickness and poverty gospel" and read between the lines for a more accurate analysis of the New Testament data. We discover that Jesus was not poor, nor were those who believed and followed him in response to the "late breaking news" of his Lordship.

By the standards of his first-century Galilean environment Jesus was relatively well off economically. When we examine the record of his first-century life and teaching it becomes obvious that he'd been able to take time to study the Scriptures in depth — time not available to a poor peasant who had to scratch for a living.

That the poor were unable to devote themselves to intense study of the Law of Moses and its current interpretation and practice is evident from Jesus' criticism of the Pharisees for laying upon the common people burdens they were unable to bear (Matthew 23:4).

Jesus was a *tekton*, not a simple carpenter but a contractor or builder. He apparently owned a substantial home in Capernaum and could make repairs when the friends of a paralyzed man let him down through the roof in the midst of the crowded house (Mark 2:1-4). Jesus had several brothers who could carry on the family business when he was away from home. There's no mention, after the account of the visit of the Magi, of the expensive gifts they brought to the child Jesus (Matthew 2:11), but perhaps these items contributed to the worth of the family's estate.

When enlisting his disciples Jesus chose men who were businessmen, including fishermen who owned or leased boats, nets, and other equipment and hired other men to work for them (Mark 1:20). One of his disciples, Levi or Matthew, was a publican who collected taxes; such men, though despised by their fellow Jews for collaborating with the Roman occupation, could become wealthy as we learn from the report of Jesus' encounter with Zacchaeus (Luke 19:2).

In their travels about Galilee and Judea to proclaim the good news of God's return to his people, Jesus and his followers maintained a treasury from which they distributed aid to the poor — an indication that they, themselves, were not the economically deprived "poor." The treasurer was Judas of whom John says, "having charge of the moneybag he used to help himself to what was put into it" (John 12:6); apparently the treasury was substantial, to the extent that Judas' pilfering did not make a noticeable dent in it. Several wealthy people, including the wife of one of King Herod's officials (Luke

8:3), accompanied Jesus' traveling mission and supported it. Presumably Levi, like Zacchaeus, gave his wealth away when he left the tax collector's booth, but may have used part of it to fund the mission.

Jesus said he had "nowhere to lay his head," not an indication of homelessness but simply the consequence of being involved in a traveling ministry. When sending his disciples out to preach the message of God's kingship he told them, "Carry no moneybag, no knapsack, no sandals" (Luke 10:4), a needless instruction unless those and similar articles were, in fact, available to them. Jesus didn't refuse the tribute paid him by the woman who lavished expensive ointment on him (Mark 14:3-9). At his crucifixion he was wearing an expensive seamless tunic the Roman soldiers didn't want to split up (John 19:23-24). Even Jesus' grave was not a pauper's grave but was provided by well-to-do men, Joseph of Arimathea and Nicodemus (John 19:38-40).

Early Christians were successful people.

Early Christians worshiped in the homes of substantial citizens such as Lydia, a dealer in expensive purple textiles (Acts 16:14-15), whose residences were large enough to accommodate an assembly. People like Paul with his entourage, or Priscilla and Aquila, could afford to travel through the Mediterranean world booking passage on merchant ships. In Ephesus Paul was able to rent the lecture hall of Tyrannus to conduct his seminars (Acts 19:9). He supported not only himself but also those serving with him through his trade as a craftsman in leather or textiles (Acts 18:3; 1 Thessalonians 2:9).[2] On his final visit to Jerusalem Paul was able to pay the

---

[2] Paul is traditionally called a "tentmaker" (*skenopoios*), but the term seems to imply leatherwork in general, and

expenses of four other men taking a vow (Acts 21:24), and when he was conducted to Caesarea the Roman governor, Felix, assumed he had enough money at his disposal to offer a bribe (Acts 24:26).

The New Testament writings are not the work of poor, uneducated peasants. They display a literary skill consistent with a high level of learning, thorough knowledge of the Hebrew Scriptures, and serious historical research. The manner in which the gospels are constructed reveals a deep theological insight into Jesus' own intent, and testifies to his intellectual brilliance in reformulating the story of Israel around his own ministry.

In the introductions to his Gospel and its second volume, The Acts of the Apostles (Luke 1:1-4; Acts 1:1), Luke implies that a wealthy patron named Theophilus underwrote the production and publication of these works. As more and more Christian writings were produced the church made use of the latest publishing technology, the book form (*codex*), instead of the unwieldy scrolls used for the Jewish Scriptures and other ancient literature. Today we would compare this to using the Internet to spread a message "gone viral," as opposed to issuing press releases to the local newspaper.

The New Testament writers, and Jesus himself, were multi-lingual, conversant with Aramaic, Hebrew, Greek (Jesus, Matthew 15:22-28), and perhaps Latin and various local languages such as Lycaonian (Acts 14:11). Paul

---

also the fabrication of tents and other items from goats' hair. Paul conducted this trade in Corinth together with his associates Aquila and Priscilla. If one asks what use tents would have in Corinth's metropolitan environment, it is said that sailors visiting the port would often stay in tents. But there was a ready market for other leather or goats' hair textiles such as the awnings erected over stalls in the marketplace for protection from the sun's heat.

had a Pharisaic education in Jerusalem under the eminent teacher Gamaliel, but was a native of Tarsus in Cilicia (Acts 22:3), the site of a prominent university. His wide exposure to Greek and Roman culture (he was a Roman citizen, Acts 22:5) is revealed in his address to the Areopagus in Athens in which he quotes two Greek writers, Epimenedes and Aratus (Acts 17:28). Paul's literary output reveals a philosophical genius that has been said to equal or surpass that of pagan thinkers of the time. He could write in Greek (Galatians 6:11) but, not being a professional scribe, employed the talents of those more skilled in penmanship such as Tertius who wrote Paul's letter to the Romans (Romans 16:22).

Jesus and the early Messiah-people were not poverty-stricken peasants, as they're sometimes portrayed, nor were they afflicted with illnesses that affected their ability to broadcast the "late breaking news" of God's victory. No person who came to Jesus for healing ever went away sick, or was told that their condition was sent from God to test them and teach them something, as the "other gospel" often suggests. Paul refers to his "thorn in the flesh" (2 Corinthians 12:7), traditionally thought to be some physical condition such as poor eyesight that inhibited his work. But a man in poor health, or with a disability, couldn't have done what Paul was able to do in traveling tirelessly throughout the eastern Mediterranean world while enduring beatings, starvation, imprisonment, shipwreck, and other hardships (2 Corinthians 11:24-27). He explains what his "thorn in the flesh" was: "a messenger of Satan to harass me" (2 Corinthians 12:7), the opposition to the gospel he encountered wherever he went.

If Jesus was "despised and rejected" in his crucifixion, this rejection came not from ordinary people but from those with a vested interest in maintaining the *status quo* in Judea (Luke 9:22). Jesus was the leader of a large, popular movement; many welcomed his message of the Lord's return to his people. As Mark reports, "the great throng heard him gladly" (Mark 12:37). The four Gospels altogether contain more than one hundred references to the large crowds that followed Jesus or gathered to hear his teaching, and to be healed of their afflictions or delivered from demonic oppression. His popularity with the people alarmed his enemies, who repeatedly couldn't arrest him for fear of the multitudes (e.g., Matthew 21:46).

Preachers sometimes claim that the crowds that welcomed Jesus into Jerusalem on what we call Palm Sunday had turned against him by the end of that week, but that's inaccurate; the scornful Friday crowd was a different crowd stirred up by Jesus' opponents. Even as he was being led to Golgatha, Luke tells us, "there followed him a great multitude of the people and of women who were mourning and lamenting for him" (Luke 23:27). What Jesus did was widespread public knowledge (Acts 2:22; 10:38); as Paul later reminded the Roman governor Festus and the Jewish King Herod Agrippa II "this has not been done in a corner" (Acts 26:26).

Suffering in the New Testament is persecution, not deprivation.

While the New Testament refers to the suffering of believers, that suffering is *not poverty and sickness but persecution*, because the message of the earliest Christians ran counter to prevailing societal norms. Among Jews the inclusion of Gentiles threatened the exclusivist, revolutionary mentality of the Pharisees and others, about which Jesus warned them (Luke 13:1-5). Acknowledging Jesus as Lord threatened the Jewish understanding of monotheism, and it's clear that early Christians, while not abandoning monotheism, blended the work of Jesus into the activity of the Father (1 Corinthians 8:6; see also Jesus' words in John 14:9 and elsewhere). In the Roman world the announcement that Jesus is Lord threatened the totalitarian regime of Caesar and the worship of pagan deities. For these reasons the activity of the followers of Jesus was accompanied by persecution.

Jesus stated that "there is no one who has left house or brothers or sisters or mother or father or children or lands, for my sake and for the gospel, who will not receive a hundredfold now in this time, houses and brothers and sisters and mothers and children and lands, with persecutions, and in the age to come eternal life" (Mark 10:29-30). *Jesus' followers will prosper* despite the threat of persecution from forces opposed to his message. But in what we call the Lord's Prayer he taught them to pray that they wouldn't be subject to *peirasmos*, the testing of persecution (Matthew 6:13).

When Paul speaks of "sharing Jesus' suffering" (Philippians 3:10) he's referring to the persecution that took Jesus to the cross. But this sharing (*koinonia*) doesn't mean we necessarily suffer in the same way. Rather, through baptism into Jesus we *enter into the suffering he has already undergone* for the rescue of his people. Paul says of Jesus that "though he was rich, yet for your sake he became poor, so that you by his poverty might become rich" (2 Corinthians 8:9). Interpreting this statement exclusively in a spiritual or non-material sense ignores the Lord's concern for the material welfare of his people, a concern evident in Jesus' stated mission "to proclaim good news to the poor" (Luke 4:18). The "sickness and poverty gospel" nullifies the suffering of Jesus on our behalf. It claims *we* must willingly suffer illness or economic deprivation in order to be true Christians. But if we imagine we have to suffer for ourselves, we've fallen into a "gospel" of works instead of grace.

No one would deny that Christians today in many lands are persecuted and martyred for their faith, as were believers in the early centuries of the church. Paul lists the punishing and humiliating conditions he personally endured as a missionary for the gospel (2 Corinthians 11:23-28), in a kind of reverse parody of the the self-congratulatory inscriptions Roman officials would erect to memorialize their achievements. Indeed, it was through the abuse, injury, and even violent death that Paul and other Christian leaders confronted that the gospel of Jesus, the crucified yet risen Messiah, made its way through the Roman world. As one historian comments, the suffering of these witnesses absorbed and sapped the energy of evil's opposition to the *euanggelion*, enabling that message to go forward.[3]

But the New Testament isn't the final stage in God's plan for his people; it records how the message of the Lordship of Jesus was first proclaimed and spread throughout the Mediterranean world, a transitional phase in the propagation of the good news. Nor is our era the end of the story — contrary to those who insist our time is the "end time," when Scripture makes it clear that the "last days" began when the news of Jesus' resurrection was first announced to the Jewish world (Acts 2:17). The story of Jesus' victory over "the present evil age" is still being played out. As to the time when God's plan will be consummated in history, Jesus cautioned his disciples that "no one knows, not even the angels in heaven, nor the Son, but only the Father" (Mark 13:32).

The New Testament expresses the vision for the greater culmination yet to come: "Thy will be done on earth, as it is in heaven" (Matthew 6:10). Paul declares that "every knee should bow . . . and every

---

[3] N. T. Wright, *Paul: A Biography* (HarperCollins, 2018).

tongue confess that Jesus the Messiah is Lord" (Philippians 2:10-11, citing Isaiah 45:23). The Revelation to John promises that God "will wipe away every tear from their eyes, and death shall be no more" (Revelation 21:4, citing Isaiah 25:8). These were not realities achieved in the New Testament era, except by anticipation in the new-creation community of the church. The rule of God, and the Son of God, is like seed that takes root and eventually spreads throughout the earth (Matthew 13:31). The early church labored under great difficulty, but that difficulty was not supposed to last forever.

God has better plans for this world.

Where did the idea come from that there's something evil about the material world, and we shouldn't seek to be prosperous or successful in it? Proponents of the "other gospel" often condemn worldliness, by which they mean preoccupation with things of the material world. But if the material world God made is "very good" it's appropriate to be involved in it, working out our vocation to "be fruitful and multiply and fill the earth and subdue it" (Genesis 1:22). In speaking of the "world" (*kosmos*) the New Testament writers refer not to the earth as a material entity but to *world culture* with its godless values.[4] It's of that world that Jesus speaks when he tells his disciples, "In the world you will have tribulation. But take heart; I have overcome the world" (John 16:33).

_____

[4] Especially in the Gospel of John, the "world" isn't the physical globe but the prevailing culture of the Judean religious establishment that rejected Jesus as the Son of God. This is evident from the biblical phenomenon of literary parallelism, where one line states a premise and the following line restates it in different, but corresponding, terms. In John 18:20 Jesus answers the high priest, "I

Scripture proclaims that "God is love" (1 John 4:8), or commitment to his agreement with us; the Hebrew word is *hesed*, faithfulness to the covenant; the corresponding Greek word is *agape*. If we say God puts illness, poverty, or strife of any sort upon us — or willingly permits them — for some reason known only to him, aren't we then saying that *love* made us sick or *love* made us poor or *love* put us under stress of some kind? If we consider God our Father, as do Jesus and the writers of the New Testament, what parent would wish, or inflict, such things upon his children?

It's a mistake to claim that, since "God is in control," bad things that happen must somehow be his doing. Scripture itself indicates that *God does not control everything*, since he has entrusted the management of this world to people made in his image (Genesis 1:28; Psalm 115:16). Devastating events or hurtful conditions that mar the welfare and happiness of human beings can usually be attributed to the actions and practices of people who refuse to bring their lives into line with the framework of God's covenant.

The Bible makes it clear that poverty, sickness, discord and the like are not God's doing, nor his tempting or testing us. They're the work of the enemy of God's people

---

have spoken openly to the world. I have always taught in synagogues and in the temple, where all Jews come together." By parallelism we see that when John uses the term "world" he's referring to the religious structure of his Jewish environment. The physical globe we call earth is not in question. This has interesting implications for understanding a favorite verse of Scripture, John 3:16: "For God so loved the *world* . . ." The world in focus here isn't the world of all humanity, but the world of Jesus' heritage in Israel and to which he came as "his own people" (John 1:11), although the majority didn't receive him.

and arise from disregard for God and his ways. The New Testament's "late breaking news" equips the believer to do battle against them.

Indeed, two millennia of history reveal the beneficial impact of Christian faith as a message of healing, prosperity, and justice. Regions of the world dominated by Christian influence have seen the development of hospitals and charitable organizations, institutions for research and learning, and efforts to promote the public good to an extent not seen elsewhere. The rights of the individual, valued by God as a creature in his own image, have become a cornerstone of Western culture leading to such milestones as the abolition of slavery. Industrial initiative and the results of technology have, on the whole, benefited people across the spectrum of society. Poverty has diminished, pestilence has been curbed, and people have been set free to explore their possibilities in life to a degree not seen in parts of the world where the New Testament's *euangelion* hasn't been promulgated.[4] The effect of Christianity through twenty centuries has been to "destroy the works of the devil."

In a world awash in poverty, illness, injustice, and all forms of oppression one wonders why any Christian wouldn't choose to preach a gospel of deliverance from these evils. Jesus, our great King, has already undergone the suffering that releases from the grip of evil, taking the curses of the covenant upon himself for the rescue of his people. The "late breaking news" of Jesus' Lordship over all things is "the power of God for salvation," the power to set people free from bondage to a corrupt and dehumanizing world culture.

----

[4] For a summary of the cultural and social impact of the spread of Christian faith see John Ortberg, *Who Is This Man?* (Zondervan, 2012).

Chapter 5
How the Gospel Works

Exactly *how* does Jesus "save"? Just how is the *euangelion* "the "power of God for salvation to everyone who believes, to the Jew first and also to the Greek," as Paul asserts (Romans 1:16)?

Explanations of the "how" seem to concentrate on Jesus' death as the price paid to ransom the believer from the consequence of sin, or disobedience or indifference to the Lord and his ways. Certainly the New Testament strikes this note, as when Jesus tells his followers he had come "not to be served but to serve, and to give his life as a ransom for many" (Mark 10:45), or when Paul declares that "at the right time Christ died for the ungodly" (Romans 5:6).

But if that were all there was to the gospel we'd never grasp the full picture of God's purpose in restoring his creation, the picture glimpsed throughout Scripture and portrayed dramatically on the Bible's final pages. Moreover, without the historical context of what the Lord's purpose was in calling Israel to serve him we'd never understand exactly what was accomplished, and how, when Israel's Messiah was crucified and rose again.

Explanations that focus on the death of Jesus as enacting some transaction between God and a believing person raise more questions than they answer. Where does that transaction occur — in some invisible, spiri-

tual realm opaque to the everyday life of human beings? That hardly seems consistent with the pattern of
common life we detect in the New Testament community, or with the Lord's concern for the world he made.
What does the transaction imply — that God is "out to
get us" unless someone buys him off? That doesn't
square with the Bible's portrait of the God who reaches
out to enter into a gracious agreement with people that
will bless their life, and who asks, "Have I any plea-
sure in the death of the wicked, declares the Lord GOD,
and not rather that he should turn from his way and
live?" (Ezekiel 18:23).

Truly, the death of Jesus is a "ransom." But that act
of self-giving on his part makes sense within the context
of God's long-range purpose for the creation he loves
and to which he's committed himself, a creation that
"waits with eager longing for the revealing of the sons
of God" (Romans 8:19) even as we, being believers, an-
ticipate "the redemption of our bodies" (Romans 8:23).
The cross of Jesus, and the empty tomb that followed,
aren't just things that happened so you and I can escape this vale of tears and go to heaven. These events
changed the course of human history, pointing it in a
different direction. That's the "late breaking news" of
the New Testament's *euangelion*.

The gospel changes our worldview.

For one thing, this gospel is meant to change our
worldview or mindset. That's essentially what it means
to be "born again," or "born from above" (John 3:16).
The first public announcement of Jesus' resurrection,
Peter's address to the Jews assembled in Jerusalem for
the feast of Pentecost, is an appeal to them to alter their
way of thinking about Jesus and what God is doing
through him. "Repent [*metanoesate*, change your minds]

and be baptized every one of you in the name of Jesus the Messiah for the forgiveness of your sins" (Acts 2:38).

Instead of being focused inwardly, and sinfully, on their status as God's special people the Jewish community is to recognize that the risen Messiah has restored their vocation to reach out to all peoples, the calling given to their father Abraham (Genesis 12:2-3). For many Jews of the first century this was a radical reversal in how they'd viewed their world. Peter's words echo Jesus' initial announcement of the Lord's return to his people: "Repent and believe in the gospel" (Mark 1:15), change your outlook on life and expect God, the great King, to show up once again.

The appeal to change our way of thinking, viewing the world in a new way, is a theme that permeates the New Testament writings. Through "the renewal of your mind" (Romans 12:2) believers learn to consider all things within the framework of Jesus' resurrection life. Paul appeals to the Philippians to "have this mind among yourselves, which is yours in Messiah Jesus" (Philippians 2:5), the mindset of serving others and looking to their interests. "We have the mind of the Messiah," Paul writes to the Corinthians (1 Corinthians 2:16), so we can understand the revelation that comes to us from the Lord and aren't limited by the values our corrupted culture would impose on us. Looking at reality in a different way, he says, "we destroy arguments and every lofty opinion raised against the knowledge of God, and take every thought captive to obey the Messiah" (2 Corinthians 10:5).

Of course, a complete and shocking reversal of worldview had occurred for Paul himself, known as Saul in his Jewish environment, when the risen Jesus confronted him on the road to Damascus (Acts 9:1-9). He could personally testify to how the news of Jesus' resurrection, and his authority over all things, can produce a radical alteration in the new believer's mindset or way of thinking.

Salvation, in the Bible, is rescue or deliverance from some harmful situation. (The Hebrew word is *yeshu'ah*, from which the name *Jesus* is derived; the Greek word is *soteria*.) Salvation is, in the first instance, rescue from the warped mentality of "the present evil age." It does little good to say, "I accept Jesus as my Lord and Savior," and then go on as before holding the same values and performing the same actions and, in particular, absenting oneself from the church — the community in which the new-creation worldview is supposed to be lived out. Having a person repeat a "sinner's prayer" and then telling them they're "born again" falls short of the method of New Testament evangelism. Indeed, we might admonish the person to "get into a good church that teaches the Word," but that advice regards the church simply as an instrument for instruction in Christian living. While the church ought to be that, in the New Testament the church is much more.

The Christian community isn't just a sounding board for the gospel message; *it is the message* for it's the venue where the renewed mind in response to Jesus' resurrection and authority begins to be worked out in its members' lives. The new believer is "born again through the living and abiding word of God," as Peter writes. But the context of that new birth is "obedience to the truth for a sincere brotherly love, [loving] one another earnestly from a pure heart" (1 Peter 1:22-23) — strongly implying the presence of a supportive community nurturing the new Christian in a worldview that runs counter to the one of which he has repented. That few local congregations in our Western culture put this new worldview into effect is the result of centuries of bombardment by the "other gospel," which muffles the "late breaking news" that changed the culture of the ancient Mediterranean world.

The great King's treaty with us is designed to actualize our repentance, our new worldview, through specific behaviors that respond to the revelation of his victory over death. We've seen how the instructions of Jesus, "all that I have commanded you" (Matthew 28:20), correspond to the stipulations of the treaty structure of Deuteronomy and other Scriptural examples of covenant making and covenant renewal.

In announcing God's return to his people Jesus lays out principles of behavior we might call "laws of the kingdom of God," principles that tend toward prosperous and successful living. These principles operate in the same nexus of act and consequence we find in the Hebrew Scriptures, where Israel's faithfulness to the Lord is set forth as the key to enjoying his blessing and avoiding the calamitous effects of the curse. We will examine a few of these principles.[1]

The commandment of love (agape) is primary.

Jesus' primary commandment, as we have noted, is the command to his disciples to show love for one another within their fellowship, a directive uttered several times during his final discourse (John 13:34-35; 15:12, 17). Although Jesus spoke in Aramaic, the language of first-century Jews of Galilee and Judea, John's gospel renders the word in Greek as *agape*, which doesn't mean what we usually mean by the word "love" in English. In Western culture love typically signifies an attraction toward someone, or something, and a desire to possess or enjoy the object of that attraction. The meaning of *agape*, by contrast, is more along the lines of *commitment or loyalty* to the object of love, a commitment that works toward the best interests of the people one loves.

---

[1] A fuller exposition of eight "laws of the kingdom" is provided in Pat Robertson and Bob Slosser, *The Secret Kingdom* (Thomas Nelson, 1982).

The New Testament usage of *agape* corresponds to the term *hesed* in the Hebrew Scriptures, a word used to denote the Lord's faithfulness to his covenant partners. Thus in granting his covenant to Israel the Lord proclaims himself to be "a God merciful and gracious, slow to anger, and abounding in steadfast love [*hesed*] and faithfulness" (Exodus 34:6).

The biblical worshiper can call upon the Lord for help in times of distress not because he's worthy, or because he exhibits some attractive feature the Lord wishes to reward, but simply because the Lord is faithful to the treaty he has granted his own. The Psalms, for example, abound with such appeals to the Lord's *hesed*, as in Psalm 6:4 "Turn, O Lord, deliver my life; save me for the sake of your *hesed*." Further examples of this expression are too numerous to cite here.

The love, or faithfulness and commitment, manifested among members of the new-creation community is directly dependent on the structure of the biblical covenant, not only as a primary command of the great King but also as the Lord's own motive in granting his treaty with us at the outset. We exhibit *agape* within our common life (*koinonia*) because, as John points out, the Lord has first manifested that same faithfulness toward us (1 John 4:19). Thus the New Testament contains repeated reminders to live out that *agape* in mutual forgiveness and concern. Adopting this lifestyle is the evidence that the believer is a participant in the resurrection of Jesus; as John puts it, "We know that we have passed out of death into life, because we love the brothers" (1 John 3:14).

Teaching his disciples how to pray, Jesus pointedly states that unless they forgive others for the wrongs inflicted upon them they can't know God's forgiveness for themselves (Matthew 6:15). Paul urges his Ephesian readers "to walk in a manner worthy of the calling to which you have been called, with all humility and gentleness, with patience, bearing with one another in love" (Ephesians 4:1-2). The "law of the Messiah" requires what Paul advises the believers of Philippi, "In humility count others more significant than yourselves. Let each of you look not only to his own interests, but also to the interests of others" (Philippians 2:3-4). In the Bible's treaty structure the partners of the great King are obligated to be faithful to one another as well as to their Lord.

God's love, then — his *agape* or *hesed* — is operative within his covenant, or treaty, with those he has called to partner with him in realizing the life of his new creation. "Unconditional love," so often celebrated by Christian preachers, isn't a biblical concept. God's love, in the biblical sense, operates within the framework of the covenant, and whoever steps outside that framework — or refuses to enter it to begin with — can't know God's love in its fullness.

Out of care for his creation God *provides* for every creature. Jesus illustrates God's perfection, or completeness, in pointing out that he sends his sunshine or nourishing rain upon all regardless of their merits (Matthew 5:45). But it's a mistake to say, as so many unbelievers and even Christians do, that God *loves* everyone, confusing his *providence* with his *love*. He loves those who are in communion with him: "Gather to me my faithful ones [*hasidim*], who made a covenant with me by sacrifice!" (Psalm 50:5). The world God loves is not the globe with its population but "the Israel of God" (Galatians 6:16), the community he's called to serve him.[2] The gospel's purpose is to extend membership in that Israel to all people, that they

---

[2] See the comment in Chapter 4, footnote 4.

should finally know God's love and reflect it in their dealings with one another.

Prosperity and healing depend on a posture of generosity.

Another covenantal directive of the great King is the command to be generous with one's material substance, accompanied by the promise that such generosity will be rewarded by prosperity. As Jesus states, "Give, and it will be given to you. Good measure, pressed down, shaken together, running over, will be put into your lap. For with the measure you use it will be measured back to you" (Luke 6:38). Paul states the principle this way: "Whoever sows sparingly will also reap sparingly, and whoever sows bountifully will also reap bountifully" (2 Corinthians 9:6).

Their words echo the repeated admonitions to this effect in the Book of Proverbs. "Whoever is generous to the poor lends to the LORD, and he will repay him for his deed" (Proverbs 19:17). Moreover, the greedy person who accumulates wealth for himself, giving no thought to the needs of others, will lose that wealth to someone who exercises better stewardship of the Lord's blessing. "Whoever multiplies his wealth by interest and profit gathers it for him who is generous to the poor" (Proverbs 28:8).

The purpose of accumulating wealth is not to luxuriate in opulence but to have the resources to distribute to those in need and to undergird the mission of proclaiming the good news of the Lordship of the Messiah. Jesus and his disciples maintained a treasury for these purposes. As we've seen, the young church included people of wealth whom Paul commends for their generosity, the exercise of which is a spiritual gift: "Having gifts that differ according to the grace given to us, let us use them: . . . the one who contributes, in generosity" (Romans 12:6, 8).

While Jesus made it clear that excessive concern for wealth could be a hindrance to receiving the good news of God's rule (Matthew 13:22), he also promised a "hundredfold" material reward for his followers in the "age to come" (Mark 10:29-31), the age of the new creation inaugurated in his resurrection. He also told a parable about faithful servants who used what they were entrusted with for material gain (Matthew 25:14-23). The use of our wealth to advance the "late breaking news" and to aid those who need our financial assistance is an extension of the command to love, for it gives concrete expression to it.

Christian leaders often promote tithing, or giving ten percent of one's income, to Christian ministries. They quote Malachi 3:10 where the Lord states, "Bring the full tithe into the storehouse," and then promises "a blessing until there is no more need." Tithing is consistent with the New Testament's admonitions regarding generosity, for it establishes a recurrent pattern of giving in proportion to our income that promotes a prosperous life. Biblical tithing, however, includes assisting the poor and forgotten members of the community as well as supporting institutions devoted to ministry.[3] Whether or not one spe-

---

[3] The tithe in Israel wasn't the same practice as that found in today's church. In the economy of ancient Israel coinage was scarce, and most commerce was carried on "in kind." As Malachi's words make clear the tithe was not money but a tenth of the grain harvest, which was to be brought to the house of the Lord so there would be food for the priests serving at the altar. The priestly tribe of Levi, having no farmland of its own, depended on the agricultural production of other Israelites. But the Levites weren't the only recipients of the tithe. In the covenant sequence of Deuteronomy, Moses directs Israel to give the tithe "to the Levite, the sojourner, the fatherless, and the widow"

cifically designates a tenth of his income for these causes, consistent generosity remains a mandate of the great King's agreement with us and includes the promise of blessing and economic success in life.

Still, the Lord is looking not just for financial liberality but for the offering of our whole person, "to present your bodies as a living sacrifice, holy and acceptable to God, which is your spiritual worship" — *logikein latreian*, actually "logical" or "reasonable service" (Romans 12:1). Being generous with our whole selves incorporates more than financial giving, though it certainly includes it. The biblical view of the person, or "soul" (*nefesh, psyche*), incorporates everything pertaining to a person's life including his family, reputation, and property, "not part of man, but man as a totality with a peculiar stamp."[4]

The covenant's directive to give liberally from our livelihood in order to bless others and advance the gospel message is accompanied by the promise of receiving blessing in return. In the Enlightenment worldview of scientific materialism, which excludes the operation of forces not accessible to physical de-

_____

(Deuteronomy 26:12). Indeed, according to other directives in Deuteronomy, worshipers traveling to the sanctuary to observe the annual festivals were allowed to eat from the tithe themselves, "whatever your appetite craves" (Deuteronomy 14:22-26). This is not the same practice as the tithing advocated today where the "storehouse" of Malachi, a literal granary, is reinterpreted as the ministry through which the believer is being nurtured in the faith. The New Testament doesn't repeat the command to tithe; its only reference to tithing as a regular activity occurs in Jesus' negative comments on the self-serving practices of the Pharisees (Matthew 23:23).

[4] Johannes Pedersen, *Israel: Its Life and Culture* (Copenhagen, 1926), volume I.

tection, such a command seems counterintuitive. Nevertheless one of the "laws of the kingdom," the "law of reciprocity," is at work here. As Isaac Newton's third law of motion states, "For every action there is an equal and opposite reaction." This physical principle is a model for what happens when we obey the Lord's command to be generous.

In 1948 Norbert Wiener published his theory of cybernetics, the idea that events are controlled by an information loop that includes more than the acting instrument. When we put our car on cruise control its speed is governed by a feedback loop that includes not only the cruise control setting but also the amount of fuel injected, the engine's revolutions-per-minute, road and wind resistance, and any other factors involved.

Using this analogy we can understand how our action in giving to others, and to the work of ministry, is part of a larger circle in which other factors, and other actors, come into play as part of the "loop." Our generous initiative, which itself is a response to God's prior blessing in our lives, sets in motion a process through which the benefits of prosperity return to us.

The same principle applies to our relationships with others. How people act toward us depends, in part, on how we behave toward them in a constant circle of feedback. If that circle is dysfunctional, spiraling downward toward dishonest dealings and ruptured relationships, insight from the Word of God allows us to break free of the conventional pattern imposed on us by the faulty worldview of materialism. We can introduce new information into the cybernetic loop so healing can begin. Jesus put the principle this way: "For with the judgment you pronounce you will be judged, and with the measure you use it will be measured to you" (Matthew 7:2).

Our words shape the environment we live in.

We build the world we live in through the words we speak, or the words we accept. The Bible begins with the account of God's creation of the universe through speaking. "Let there be light," he said, and light came into being (Genesis 1:3). Psalm 33 echoes the Genesis narrative: "By the word of the LORD the heavens were made, and by the breath of his mouth all their host" (Psalm 33:6). As creatures made in the image of God human beings have the same power to shape the environment in which they live. For this reason the careful and creative use of speech is a mandate for those bound to the Lord in his agreement we call the covenant. Words can build up, and words can also destroy.

God's treaty, itself, is called his Word. Indeed what we call the Ten Commandments, the heart of Deuteronomy's covenant structure, aren't called commandments in Hebrew; they're called "the ten words" (*devarim*, Deuteronomy 4:13). The New Testament calls Jesus the Word (*logos*) of God (John 1:1, 14; Revelation 19:13) because he's the Son through whom the Father has inaugurated his new creation and, indeed, through whom he initially brought the universe into being (John 1:3, Hebrews 1:2). Through Jesus the Son, God spoke to us in "these last days," and the Son continues to "uphold the universe [*ta panta*, everything] by the word of his power" (Hebrews 1:3). The way the New Testament describes the impact of Jesus as the Word underscores the stress the Scriptures place on the importance of words.

Please allow us a brief detour into the realm of the science of physics. It may be that, ultimately, all things are made up of words and not "hard stuff." The deeper researchers probe the constituency of matter the more elusive that matter appears to be, so that particles of matter (protons, neutrons, electrons) once held to be "basic stuff" making up the atom break down into other entities that give them their properties, as mentioned earlier.

General relativity is a theory that applies to larger objects and involves gravity, while quantum field theory applies to particles at the subatomic level and attempts to reconcile the universe's three non-gravitational forces: the "weak" and "strong" nuclear forces and electromagnetism. However, these two theories are incompatible and both can't be correct. To reconcile them into a "theory of everything" some physicists have proposed that all basic entities of matter are "strings," not "stuff" at all but vibrating strands with particular frequencies, and that the frequencies determine the nature of the different particles.[5]

A word is a communication of some sort, a piece of information. But information is "a difference that makes a difference," since there's no information in undifferentiated sameness.[6] Communication of these informational differences typically involves frequencies, whether those of transmitted electromagnetic waves detectable by instruments such as radios or cellular phones or the vibrations of human vocal chords, loudspeakers, or other sources.

It's easy to see, by analogy with the vibrations or frequencies of string theory, why Scripture can speak of the *word* as the foundational building block of all reality, the *logos* through which the universe came into being and which sustains it. Cosmic background radiation, first discovered in 1965, pervades the universe and is considered the echo of the "big bang" that brought

---

[5] The author is by no means an expert in this field of study, but must rely on sources that have the stamp of credibility.
[6] Gregory Bateson, *Steps to an Ecology of Mind* (Chandler Publishing, 1972).

the universe into being. Psalm 19 seems to describe this phenomenon, as viewed from a geocentric perspective:

The heavens declare the glory of God,
and the sky above proclaims his handiwork.
Day to day pours out speech,
and night to night reveals knowledge.
There is no speech, nor are there words,
whose voice is not heard.
Their voice goes out through all the earth,
and their words to the end of the world (Psalm 19:1-4).

"Speech" that is "no speech," or words that are "not heard," could well describe the informational frequencies that underlie the existence of all matter. In stressing the importance of words the Bible is pointing to the word-foundation of all that exists, a truth cosmologists and physicists are beginning to hint at.

Our Western culture has forgotten the power of words because it's preoccupied with visible, material substance. In Scripture the spoken word has almost the effect of a physical force. The Hebrew word *davar*, usually translated "word," in some contexts means "a thing" or "a matter." Of young Samuel, as he grew up into his vocation as a prophet, Scripture says "the Lord was with him and let none of his words fall to the ground" (1 Samuel 3:19).

The Bible consistently stresses the importance of our verbal output, since what we say constructs the world we live in. As Proverbs puts it, "From the fruit of a man's mouth his stomach is satisfied; he is satisfied by the yield of his lips. Death and life are in the power of the tongue, and those who love it will eat its fruits" (Proverbs 18:20-21).

We get what we say; speaking positively yields beneficial results, but negative speech brings about the opposite result. A parent who consistently tells their child, "You just make trouble for us, you'll never amount to anything," will soon grieve over the poor choices of their teenager or young adult. The person who complains, "I get the flu every year at this time," is likely to be laid up for a while. If we're careless with our speech we can be "snared in the words of [our] mouth" (Proverbs 6:2), and through the nexus of act and consequence we might experience some of the unsavory conditions mentioned in the curses of the covenant. Let's not get "hung by our tongue."

On the other hand, when we speak in agreement with our great King's covenant promise of protection and blessing with the expectation that the Lord will be faithful to his agreement with us, we're more likely to prosper and enjoy good health. Stress is recognized as a major factor in the onset of disease; speaking positively about our situation can reduce our stress level as we hear ourselves voicing a hopeful outlook.

Jesus, when instructing his disciples how to confront the "mountain" blocking their way, didn't tell them to pray to God about the obstacle; he told them to *speak to the mountain* (Mark 11:23). A woman suffering from a hemorrhage was healed because, in faith, *"she said*, 'If I touch even his garments, I will be made well'" (Mark 5:28). Jesus underscored the critical role our words have in shaping our life and environment: "I tell you, on the day of judgment people will give account for every careless word they speak, for by your words you will be justified, and by your words you will be condemned" (Matthew 12:36-37).

The same cybernetic loop through which our attitude of generosity results in a life of prosperity is operative in our vocal activity. Speaking out the promises of the Word of God initiates a feedback process that brings the blessing of the Lord back to us. As people made in the image of God we have our own measure of the same word-power he has when he declares, "So shall my word be that goes out from my mouth; it shall not return to me empty, but it shall accomplish that which I purpose, and shall succeed in the thing for which I sent it" (Isaiah 55:11).

The gospel of Jesus' authority is the "prosperity gospel."

The principles we have cited here — the command of loving commitment to members of God's family; the directive to be generous with our substance; and the emphasis on the power of the spoken word — are only three of the "laws of the kingdom" through which the gospel works to bring healing, prosperity, and harmony into our lives. These principles follow from the "late breaking news" that Jesus, risen from the dead, has brought God's new creation into being, has taken authority over all things, and is at work to bring justice to this world.

This *euangelion*, the good news of Jesus' rule and how the great King's treaty with us functions for our benefit, has been labeled the "prosperity gospel" or "health and wealth gospel." In certain Christian circles it has been much maligned. An Internet search will turn up a plethora of web sites, blogs, and the like raising objections to the idea that following Jesus leads to a healthier, more prosperous life. The assumption of these critics is that the Christian life is to be marked by suffering, so that Jesus-followers who view their faith as promoting prosperity and health are departing from the pattern of the New Testament church.

Even otherwise astute scholars of the New Testament have been heard to state that the "prosperity gospel" is only a way for rich Americans to justify their lifestyle of consumption. That's a conclusion based on a misunderstanding of prosperity teaching, and one hardly justified by the biblical evidence for the nexus of act and consequence and the promises inherent in the covenant.

We hope we've presented enough of this evidence to counter such claims, and to call into question the objections of those critics who would instead advocate a "sickness and poverty gospel." The gospel of Jesus was "good news to the poor." The message of Paul was that the curses of sickness, poverty, and oppression spelled out in the Bible's covenant pattern have been borne by the Messiah on the cross, and are not the inevitable lot of God-fearing humanity. This is the New Testament's "late breaking news": that Jesus, raised from the dead and living now, has the authority of the Son of God to govern the affairs of humankind through his gracious agreement with us, and through living out its provisions we, together with him, are destroying the works of the enemy.

Appendix
What Kind of God?

In the preceding chapters we've laid out the major implications of the New Testament's "late breaking news." Because the Son of God, the great King, has all authority we share an appropriate measure of that authority as his treaty partners. This is a compelling picture, but let's remind ourselves that it's an image couched in the perspective of a document coming to us from the world of two or more millennia ago. The portrayal of God in the Scriptures doesn't have the sort of shape that dovetails with the way most people see their world today.

To an observer standing on the surface of the earth it looks like the starry night sky is a great dome covering the land area. As the new day dawns the sun appears in the east, then circles beneath the dome of the sky and sets in the west as the stars begin to reappear. Because this is how the universe really appears to an earth-dweller with no access to astronomical instruments and no knowledge of the findings of several centuries of scientific study of the universe, we would call this a geocentric perspective.

From this viewpoint the sun and other bodies in the sky revolve around the earth. The "heavens" are "up" above the land and perhaps some kind of shadowy underworld lies below. Until the work of Copernicus (sixteenth century) and Galileo (seventeenth century) this geocentric perspective was sustained even among astronomers, for whom the old system of epicycles devised by the second-century Egyptian astronomer Ptolemy worked quite well to explain the movements of the heavenly bodies.

The Bible is written from a geocentric perspective.

The geocentric viewpoint is the world-perspective from which the authors of Scripture write. The events of the creation are pictured in a manner consistent with the standpoint of an earthly observer, with the dome of the sky, or firmament, separating the habitable land area where people live from a watery space above. The firmament is heaven, or at least a level of heaven (because the atmosphere is also a level of heaven), and God and his hosts are portrayed as dwelling "up" in that realm above the earth.

When God chooses to interact with people, he must in some manner come "down" to meet them. Because that's the way people saw their world, it would have made no sense to them to speak otherwise about God. Whether or not the Scriptural writers had a different picture of the cosmos in their minds, they had a more important message to convey than straightening out peoples' thinking about the structure of the physical universe.

In Western or Western-influenced cultures, at least, the rise of astronomy, physics, and other sciences since the eighteenth century and the popularization of their findings have changed the picture most people have of the universe. We know the sky is not heaven, and God does not live "up there." We know the earth is a tiny dot in a vast universe of uncounted billions of galaxies populated by untold trillions of stars and other bodies. When Yuri Gagarin, the first Soviet cosmonaut, returned to earth in 1961 the Soviet Premier, Nikita Khrushchev, proclaimed triumphantly that his atheism was vindicated because Gagarin had not seen God up there. "Well, duh," we might be tempted to exclaim.

The Bible's geocentric perspective is still with us. Weather broadcasters announce when the sun will "rise" and "set" the next day. One can empathize with the old farmer who observed, "They say the earth goes around the sun, but I know different because I see the sun come up in the east in the morning and go down in the west at night." Although we know, from the results of science, that the global earth revolves in orbit about the sun and the sky is not a solid dome but a window into an infinite space viewed from the surface of our tiny planet, we still speak this way. We celebrate sunrises and sunsets as things of beauty without stopping to consider that such beauty is merely the result of the refraction of sunlight through water vapor in the atmosphere, as viewed from our particular location and appreciated in our own mind. Even in the world of the Internet, the "up and down" geocentric perspective holds forth; we speak of uploading and downloading data, and of the "cloud" of available resources. Yes, a transmission satellite may be above the user from a certain location, but most data resides on a server somewhere on the surface of the earth.

Still, for many people immersed in the worldview of scientific materialism the biblical picture of God can be an obstacle to faith. It doesn't help the situation when Christians continue to speak of God, pray to him, and worship him as though he's like "a big angel up in the sky" (to borrow Frank Turek's phrase).

When Christians advocate the truth of God and his plan for human life, including the lifestyle standards he lays out in his Word, the typical "Christianese" in which they express themselves may leave unbelievers unimpressed. After all, they reason, Christians are just blindly parroting the opinions of benighted souls who lived in a dark, pre-scientific age and thought they had heard from some supernatural Source who really isn't there — but now we know so much more than they did! This is the stranglehold the Enlightenment has upon the thinking of most people in the West and many others the world over. To them the Bible has nothing to say that's applicable to the kind of universe we live in today, and its witness can be discounted and ignored.

So, although the biblical authors typically write from a geocentric perspective and we understand why they needed to do that, it may be time to learn some new ways of thinking and speaking about God that are consistent with Scripture but not so susceptible to Khrushchev's inane comment or the general skepticism of our prevailing culture. Instead of going "high" we must go "deep." It should be made evident that the Scriptural authors had a more sophisticated perception of reality than the flat, materialistic view that modernity imposes upon us. The biblical witness needs to be related to what cosmologists and atomic physicists are finding out about the nature of the universe, and what comprises it. Let's explore some possibilities along these lines.

Scripture contains hints of a perspective beyond the geocentric.

Scripture affirms that the space-time universe is a witness to the reality of its Creator. Psalm 19 opens with the declaration that the firmament, the starry sky as viewed from earth, "proclaims his handiwork." Paul picks up that thought in pointing out that the power and divinity of God "have been clearly perceived, ever since the creation of the world, in the things that have been made" (Romans 1:20). According to the consensus of cosmologists this still-expanding universe of space, time, and matter had a beginning, called the "big bang," similar to that described in the opening verses of the Book of Genesis.

The scriptural authors understood that nothing existed — not time, nor space, nor matter — when the universe came into being. The writer of Hebrews states, "By faith we understand that the universe [*aiones*, "ages" or the world as a spatial entity through time] was created by the word of God, so that what is seen was not made out of things that are visible" (Hebrews 11:3). Moreover, the Bible states that light appeared as a separate stage in creation (Genesis 1:3) after the "big bang," a concept that becomes plausible to us in terms of the theory that the plasma, or primordial matter, of the universe expanded to something much closer to its present size in the first split second after creation. It expanded faster than the speed of light, which itself had first to be differentiated from that primordial plasma that was "without form and void" (Genesis 1:2).

If a "big bang" brought the space-time universe, and then light, into being, *a decision had to be made* to set that process in motion — but decisions can only be made by a Person, of whatever nature. So God was "there when" the universe began. But if physicists are right in concluding that both time and space were created in the "big bang" it's not strictly correct to speak of a "when" or a "there." The Bible seems to think of God as beyond time and space, for he "inhabits eternity" (Isaiah 57:15) and "heaven, even highest heaven, cannot contain him" (2 Chronicles 2:6).

The biblical authors recognized that we, being four-dimensional creatures in a space-time environment, aren't able to penetrate the full reality of the One "who alone has immortality, who dwells in unapproachable

light, whom no one has ever seen or can see" (1 Timothy 6:16) — yet who, at the same time, dwells in "thick
darkness" (Exodus 20:21; 1 Kings 8:12; and elsewhere).
Israel understood that it couldn't confine the being of
God to categories easily accessible to human understanding. The Lord's divine name *Yahweh*, when revealed to
Moses (Exodus 3:14-15), is related to the Hebrew verb
hayah, "to be," in the form *'ehyeh asher 'ehyeh*, "I will be
who I will be," reflecting the mystery and inaccessibility
of his being. As Paul exclaims, "Oh, the depth of the
riches and wisdom and knowledge of God! How
unsearchable are his judgments and how inscrutable his
ways!" (Romans 11:33).

The biblical authors wrote of God from the geocentric
standpoint, speaking of the Lord's "coming down" (Genesis 11:5); of good gifts "coming down from the Father of
lights" (James 1:17); of Jesus being "lifted up" in his as-
cension to the Father; or of Paul being "caught up to the
third heaven" (2 Corinthians 12:2). But they knew very
well they were using a kind of shorthand to accommodate their message to the limits of human understanding.
We use that same shorthand today, but we need to be
prepared to explain that it's not intended as a literal description of God and his relation to the universe. More
than that, it may be a good idea to lay it aside when we're
not actually quoting from the Bible. God isn't "up there";
rather, his "space" pervades our space at all times and
everywhere, as we shall suggest below.

God operates in dimensions beyond our familiar four.

In what space, then (if we may use the word *space*
in this context), does the invisible God operate? God's
space is often called *heaven*, but as we've seen any sort
of "heaven" that refers to a spatial entity is only a meta-
phor for the realm of God's activity. We may say that

God operates in a spiritual realm, but what does that mean? Cosmology and astrophysics are helping us to understand that the visible universe (so far, for the limits of visibility keep expanding) is only about five percent of its total mass. "Dark matter" and "dark energy" comprise most of the mass of the universe — "dark" in the sense that they can't be directly detected by the instruments available to research.

Moreover, when it comes to the subatomic level even the matter that's visible is mostly space. There would be plenty of "room" for an unseen Power to operate in what we could call a spiritual manner, but we must caution that this "room" is only an analogy because the spiritual realm, or "God's space," may be in a dimension beyond the four space-time dimensions accessible to us in which the concept of "room" has meaning.

Proponents of string theory as the "theory of everything" posit that the vibrating strands whose frequencies determine the properties of the subatomic particles of matter must oscillate across multiple dimensions, not just the four dimensions accessible to us. As many as eleven dimensions have been suggested, existing at every point in the universe in a mathematical configuration known as the Calabi-Yau manifold after its formulators. If only by analogy, the possibility of dimensions beyond those we normally experience should open people to consideration of the realm of the spirit as a dimension in which God operates, usually invisible to us but sometimes blending into our familiar environment in phenomena mislabeled "miracles."

People think of such occurrences, including unexplained healing from disease, as supernatural events. Scripture, however, doesn't recognize a category called "supernatural" because it understands that God, operating in his extradimensional manner, is continually involved in the four-dimensional world of what we call "nature" or the material. The Bible affirms that God created that world in the first place. If something remarkable, with causation beyond our grasp, occurs it may be a "sign" or a "wonder" but it's not a supernatural event as far as the biblical authors are concerned.

While people steeped in the worldview of scientific materialism find it difficult to accept the reality of such unexplained events, most people in the "majority world" of Africa, Asia, and Latin America have no problem with them. Their worldview typically includes the recognition of non-material forces, for they aren't trapped in the grip of the Enlightenment.[1] Unexplained events of healing from disease or demonic oppression occur with greater frequency in the majority world because people are open to such phenomena, whereas the Western mindset rules them out of consideration.

If we were two-dimensional creatures living in "Flatland" we would know only length and width but not height. If a cube, a three-dimensional object, were placed on Flatland we would encounter it only as a square; if such an object were to cut through the plane of our two-dimensional surface we would know it only as a pattern of lines. In the same way, we who live in a four-dimensional space-time universe have trouble comprehending anything, such as the operation of God in the spirit, that intersects our world from another dimension. That from our viewpoint God dwells in "unapproachable light" is the result of the dimensional difference between our being and his.

Paul's quotation to the effect that "in him we live and move and have our being" (Acts 17:28) and his declaration that "from him and through him and to

[1] Craig S. Keener, *Miracles: The Credibility of the New Testament Accounts*, volumes I-II (Baker Academic, 2011).

him are all things" (Romans 11:36) suggest that he understood that God's being penetrates and pervades our being in a non-spatial way, so that he's never far from us. The Lord's good gifts which James says come "down from the Father of lights" can be understood non-geocentrically, emerging at every point in and around us as God's extradimensional space meshes with ours.

These considerations are food for thought when we consider the Gospel accounts of the resurrection of Jesus. While the empty tomb, the excited wonder of the first reports, and the evident proximity of those reports to the original event bear witness to the resurrection, the nature of Jesus' resurrection body remains a mystery. He appears to his followers as a normal human being, not in some halo of shining light. But at first they don't recognize him. It's only when he speaks, with his "Mary" (John 20:16), his blessing of the bread at Emmaus (Luke 24:36), or his "Peace to you" (Luke 24:36), that his followers realize who he is. Jesus can suddenly appear to his disciples in a locked room (John 20:19), yet he's able to eat a piece of broiled fish (Luke 24:42-43) and even prepare a breakfast of fish for his disciples (John 21:9-12).

Jesus' resurrection body, as the "firstborn of many brothers" (Romans 8:29), is the preview of the believers' body in God's renewed creation when "we shall be like him" (1 John 2:28). Such a body is not an immaterial body in some far-off heaven, for it merges with the space-time world; yet neither is it a body confined to the four dimensions of our familiar space. It brings our space into line with God's "space," according to his "plan for the fullness of time, to unite all things in him, things in heaven and things on earth" (Ephesians 1:10). For the body of the resurrection N. T. Wright has coined the term *transphysical*.

God communicates with us from his own "space."

In considering the specific information about God's requirements for human behavior embodied in his treaty with his partners, this question must arise: How does a spiritual, or extradimensional, Being communicate with spokesmen who are creatures of a physical, four-dimensional space-time universe? Biblical figures in both Old and New Testaments claim to have heard from the Lord and communicate the message they've received to members of their faith community. Expressions to this effect are too numerous to cite more than a few. "The word of the LORD came to me" (Jeremiah 1:13), or some similar expression, is constantly on the lips of the Hebrew prophets. Jesus declares, "I have not spoken on my own authority, but the Father who sent me has himself given me a commandment" (John 12:49). Paul differentiates between what is his personal opinion and what comes to him from the Lord (1 Corinthians 7:10). Every believer, he asserts, can know what God is thinking, for "we have the mind of the Messiah" (1 Corinthians 2:16).

The Bible's role as the sourcebook for the church's faith and practice depends on the understanding that it presents God's Word, communicated through people who heard from him and are passing his message along to us. "Men moved by the Holy Spirit spoke from God," Peter states (2 Peter 1:21 RSV). "'What no eye has seen, nor ear heard, nor the heart of man imagined, what God has prepared for those who love him —'" writes Paul quoting Isaiah 64:4, "these things God has revealed to us through the Spirit. For the Spirit searches everything, even the depths of God" (1 Corinthians 2:9-10). The extradimensional Person of God is able to intersect the thought processes of those inhabitants of the space-time universe who are open to receiving his message, despite the fact that God's thoughts are not our thoughts but far beyond them (Isaiah 55:8).

No one really understands how the firing of neurons through the synapses of the human brain's network, and the chemical reactions involved, can create memory and endow each human being with self-awareness, the sense of being "me" as opposed to other entities present in our psychological environment. Yet memory and self-awareness are the universal experience of every healthy human being.

At each moment of our day we're being bombarded with millions of waves and particles, such as those originating in solar radiation or in radio or cellular phone signals, that pass through us without colliding with any component of our physical bodies — so great is the comparative distance between the particles that make up the matter of which we're made. Is it beyond belief that the mind of the Creator communicates through this same space, and can target specific regions in the brains of his chosen spokesmen to cause them to "hear" from him in a special way — so that "men moved by the Holy Spirit spoke from God"? After all, God isn't remote, far off in some celestial heaven, as the traditional geocentric perspective portrays him, or billions of light-years away beyond the far side of an immense universe. He is in, through, and around us at all times operating in his dimensional "space" that intersects ours. The great King is fully capable of making his will known to us.

Exactly how God, out of his extradimensional "space," is able to communicate information to entities in the physical space-time universe is, and may long remain, a mystery. Nevertheless, evidence from evolutionary biology also testifies to the impact and operation of a Creator in the physical realm. The cells of all living organisms contain a kind of blueprint for the manufacture of protein, known as DNA (deoxyribonucleic acid). DNA is a sequence made up of four chemicals called nucleobases, and the variable arrangement or sequence of these nucleobases constitutes an information code replicated by a corresponding sequence of messenger RNA (ribonucleic acid) that transmits the information to where it's needed in the cell to enable the manufacture of different proteins.

Probability calculations show that such a sequential code, which includes a vast amount of information, couldn't have arisen by accident over eons of time. There aren't enough particles in the universe nor has enough time elapsed since the "big bang" to make it probable that the right components to create even a simple information code could have come together by chance. Information of this irreducible complexity can only come from a Mind or Intelligence.[2]

God communicates digitally.

Information is found in the difference between one thing and another. There's no information in a light bulb, for example, but only in the different entities the light bulb illuminates. There's no information in a blank sheet of paper except at its edges where it differs from its background. In our computers information is the difference between *on* and *off*, as the bits and bytes are modified by the system. Computer machine code is symbolized as a series of zeroes and ones: 1-0-1-0-0-1-0-1. There's no half *off* or half *on*, only one or the other which is what being digital means. If everything were the same — all *on*, for example — no information would be conveyed. We learn nothing from a blank screen, which computer geeks call the BSOD or "blue screen of death," except that something's gone wrong with the computer!

---

[2] Stephen C. Meyer, *Signature in the Cell: DNA and the Evidence for Intelligent Design* (HarperCollins, 2009).

God's Word, too, is digital; it's "the difference that makes a difference." We see this, for example, in the English Old Testament all the way from Genesis to Malachi (the Hebrew order of books is different). In Genesis God creates by making a difference. He says, "Let there be light," and divides the light from the darkness just as in a computer the bytes are either *on* or *off*. The rest of creation proceeds by a process of analysis (literally, "breakdown"), as different creatures and objects are separated from their undifferentiated background matter into what the Creator has designed for them. Creation is a digital process.

At the very end of the English Old Testament we hear the Lord saying, "Then once more you shall see the distinction between the righteous and the wicked, between one who serves God and one who does not serve him" (Malachi 3:18). That's a digital difference. The treaty of the great King is digital information. God's people will either follow him or they won't; there's no middle ground.

The oft-repeated word *if* in God's Word is comparable to the *if* or conditional symbol of a computer program flowchart, which designates an operation determining which of two paths the program will take. Jesus expresses this digital difference when he says, "Whoever is not with me is against me" (Matthew 12:30). Our faith is digital; our byte is either turned *on* or it's turned *off*. We follow the Lord to receive his blessing, but whoever departs from his way will encounter the conditions of the curse Jesus died and arose again to remove.

We hope that, in what we've presented above in analogies from the realm of science and technology, we've been able to suggest some different ways of speaking about God and how he relates to his covenant partners. We stress that these are analogies, not proofs. It's never a good move to assert that "science proves the Bible is true," as some

Christian apologists try to do. If we make that claim, then science — the authority of the Enlightenment worldview — becomes the criterion of truth.

Jesus, however, prayed to his Father affirming that "your word is truth" (John 17:17). We begin with the Word of God and his Messiah, the New Testament's "late breaking news," as the truth and then find ways to express it in a framework that can resonate with people schooled in a culture of scientific materialism. In any case, scientific "truth" itself is continually evolving as new discoveries emerge, as new theories are advanced, and more importantly as new paradigms or perspectives call earlier ones into question.[3] Science is never the final word concerning the realities we have to deal with. Rather, it's our great King, revealing his authority over all things, "to whom we must give account" (Hebrews 4:13).

---

[3] Thomas S. Kuhn, *The Structure of Scientific Revolutions*, second edition (University of Chicago Press, 1970).

www.ingramcontent.com/pod-product-compliance
Lightning Source LLC
Chambersburg PA
CBHW071831020426
42331CB00007B/1687